Her God-Sized Dream

How to Believe, Walk, and Run with It

Scripture quotations are from The Holy Bible, New International Version* Copyright ©1973, 1978, 1984 by the International Bible Society.

Printed in the United States of America
2019 First Edition

Subject Index:
Nixon, Melissa J.
Title: Her God-Sized Dream - How to Believe, Walk, & Run With It
   1.   Inspirational 2. Purpose 3. Self-Help 4. Christian

Paperback ISBN: 978-1-64085-593-9
EPub ISBN: 978-1-64085-595-3
Hardback ISBN: 978-1-64085-594-6
Library of Congress Control Number: 2019933635
Author Academy Elite, Powell Oh

courageouslifeacademy.com

This book is dedicated to every woman with a God-sized Dream!
No matter where you are in your journey, you have arrived here, for
such a time as this!

"For if you remain silent at this time, relief and deliverance for the
Jews will arise from another place, but you and your father's family will
perish. And who knows but that you have come to your royal position
for such a time as this?"
Esther 4:14

Table of Contents

Foreword

Introduction

Chapter 1: 7 Steps to Your God-Sized Dream

Chapter 2: 5 Things Getting in the Way of Your God-Sized Dream

Chapter 3: Don't Despise Small Beginnings - Lana Hunter

Chapter 4: Preparing Your Faith & Finances - Nyisha Holliday

Chapter 5: Building Your Dream While Working a 9-to-5 - Kimberly Hall

Chapter 6: Achieving Your Dream at Any Age - Joan Turley

Chapter 7: Overcoming Distractions - Cheryl Riley

Chapter 8: Activating Your Dream

Afterword

Acknowledgments

Endnote

About the Authors

Foreword

We had only been married a year or so, but we'd been together since we were 15. That's why I couldn't believe what my husband was telling me. That man looked me dead in my face, me, the girl he'd known since high school. Me, the person who spent all her summers at music camps and had told him when he proposed that I would still be going away to study piano. Me, the person who was planning to get her doctorate of piano performance right after we finished up our two - year stint in Houston so I could get my Master's in piano performance. That man looked me dead in my face and said, "I don't think piano is going to be your thing."

The side-eye was real. I don't know if he knows how close I came to leaving him that night. How dare he doubt my ability to make a career as a concert pianist? I mean, sure he'd been witness to some devastating musical experiences, some bad concerts, my disappointment over not getting into certain conservatories or programs, my not being able to understand why certain doors to the life I wanted just weren't opening, but did he really think I couldn't do it? He tried to quickly explain that what he meant was that the piano wouldn't be my *main* thing. Instead, he believed the piano would be the thing that would open important doors for me to do other important things. I didn't care about his clarification. All I heard and felt was rejection. In my mind, he was doubting me, my purpose, my future and my childhood dream.

The truth is...you don't need another book about dreams! At least, you don't need another book telling you to dream or telling you to dream big. Why? Because you've been dreaming in technicolor your whole life. In fact, you're tired of dreaming. Seriously, you're literally tired from dreaming. It's exhausting! Especially when fruition is hard to come by.

What you need, is to know the pre-requisites for seeing your dream come to pass. What you need, is to know how to partner with God and follow your dreams into fruition. What you need, is to build up that "Big Girl Panties" faith! Yup, I said that. You need to build God-Sized faith to match your God-Sized dreams.

Before you read the first chapter of this powerful book, the most difficult thing you'll have to do first is to surrender your dream. Can I even challenge you a bit more? I dare you to sacrifice your dream, literally slay that thing and lay it on the altar. Give it back to God *before* you pursue it full throttle. Most of us wait to surrender when things aren't working out as we hoped. I want you to see how much time you're about to gain when you surrender, in advance, and bypass all the detours and delays.

After you've relinquished it, and before God gives it back to you, you'll need to commit to one more thing. Commit to trading in your childhood dream for your adult-sized destiny. What that means is you'll need to come to terms with the fact that all your life you've only seen parts of the full picture. Maybe God gave you a talent like playing the piano and you ran with that, assuming your dream was to be a world-famous concert pianist. Isn't that every pianist's dream? But it's only now, much later in life, after you went and majored in music and dedicated countless hours of your life to practicing, and your husband dared to drop a nugget in your heart that would anger you at first, but eventually change your life, that you see the piano was just the vehicle to get you in unexpected rooms. That's MY story. I promise yours is similar. You've only been living out part of your dream, that part closely aligned to your gifts and talents and skills. But now? Now you're ready for the God-Sized dream, the one with purpose and destiny built into it, the one with unbelievable impact and influence.

So, like I tell the visionary women I coach who have big dreams on their heart, "breathe, believe, and buckle up!" **Breathe** because you'll need a minute to take this all in. Melissa and friends are going to inspire you. They're also going to step on your toes a bit and maybe even hurt your feelings because they haven't held back. They've been honest about what's needed if you're serious about what's next.

Believe you can do this thing. Commit to developing a passion for God's will like never before and determine to do the work attached to the assignment. Purpose in your heart that this is the new era that's been prophesied over you a million times. This is the season you'll bear fruit. Now is the time you'll run and not grow weary. Stay expectant about what's ahead, even for the trials that are readying to better prepare you for your next level. Be grateful in advance for all that's coming your way.

Buckle up because we are in an era of velocity. God is moving faster than ever before and we must keep up. As fast as the blessings and the breakthroughs will come, so will the opposition and the overwhelming feelings. It's par for the course and that's okay. But you'll need to be ready to handle it all. I pray that as things begin to open up around you, nothing you cherish will crumble or be knocked out of balance because this thing you're heading into is huge. May God grant you room in your heart, space in your brain, and the strength of spirit to be able to triumphantly carry all that He's designed you to birth. May the Holy Spirit wall this thing out with you step by step.

Now...go get your God-Sized dream!

Jade Simmons,

World-Class Concert Pianist, Powerhouse Speaker, and Author,
Audacious Prayers for World Changers
jadesimmons.com

Intro

A God-Sized Dream

*What if... we dared to trust God to bring all of our wildest
dreams to pass?*

*What... if every time a wild and crazy idea dropped into
our thinking we were full of faith and not fear?*

*What if...our mind and thoughts went to who God is,
instead of who we are?*

Do you remember the day that wild idea dropped into your
thoughts? You know the one that made your heart skip a beat,
gave you that weird feeling in the pit of your stomach, or made you gasp!
I bet you can remember exactly where you were and what you were
doing at that moment. Even if you don't, I'm positive you still remember
that rushing wind which came over you with thoughts of amazement,
excitement, and wonder but quickly followed by thoughts of
intimidation, fear, and even, "Who am I do to that? Am I crazy?"

When it first hit, I am sure your mind ran crazy with all the possibilities
of what life would be like if *it* really happened. You could see yourself
doing it, you could feel not only the excitement, but the contentment of
walking in your calling. You could feel the freedom ... the freedom to be
who you were really called to be, the freedom of time, and you even felt
the financial freedom you knew would come with your highest level of
success. After seeing what life would be like on the other side, the
magnitude of your idea either sent you into instant action, consumed
you with a ton of questions, or both. In some instances, it may have
paralyzed you with fear because it was so big and drastically different
from your current life.

If you're like me, moments of these brilliant ideas have not been a once in a lifetime occurrence. They happen throughout our life because God does not have just *one* dream for us, He has *multiple* dreams for us. He does not just want to do exceedingly and abundantly above all that we could ask, think, or imagine in *one* area of our life, but in *every* area of our lives. Dreams that He wants to help you bring to fruition, including the one that made you pick up this book.

I will never forget the day I decided to wholeheartedly pursue my dreams of becoming a speaker and an entrepreneur. Not only did the whole idea feel so much bigger than me, but it had been tugging at me for a long time. In fact, for twenty years. Some of you may remember that story from my first book, *The Courageous Life*. As much as I felt like it was the thing I was supposed to do, I did not know how to make it happen. I had never spoken anywhere outside of the company trainings I did at work. No one knew my name, and I knew nothing about running a business outside of the case studies I read in grad school. I had what I called a God-Sized dream. The type of dream where the only way it would happen is if God himself showed you how to do it. I am certain that if you are reading this book, you also have a dream or two that are bigger than you. The ones where you say, "If God doesn't do it, it will not get done!"

A God-Sized dream takes more than our own skill, our own intellect, and our own abilities. There isn't even a way we can manipulate our way into it. If we could achieve it based upon who we know, or simply buy our way into it, we would have done it a long time ago. By now, it would be something we already accomplished and not something we have to hope, wish, and pray for. Most certainly, we would not be worried about it nor sitting in fear and doubt. Or worse, watching from the sidelines as someone else is doing something similar. Even more so, regretting the fact that we could be so much further along if we did not get in our own way.

A God-Sized dream is a dream that you know requires more than your contagious passion or hard work ethic. It requires a higher power from the Lord Jesus himself to be able to come in and intervene on your behalf with the many things you're dealing with. God-Sized dreams require absolute divine interventions that only He can orchestrate and doors that only He can open.

What is it for you? Is it writing a book, but you wonder who is going to read it? Is it starting a business, but you're not sure how you will make money? Or is it going to the next level in your career, but you're not sure exactly what steps to take to get promoted? Some of you may not even be able to clearly articulate it, but you know that there is something more for you to do beyond where you are. And just like me, you have a quiet desperation for the life you know you would have if you trusted God with reckless abandon, and allowed Him to truly be the head of your life. Think of how great a shift it would be if you spent time chasing Him versus trying to hold onto the comfort you are used to. Deep down, you hear that voice of quiet desperation whispering, "there is something greater for me to do." The question then becomes, when will you do it? We wonder when will we finally learn to trust the One who gave us the dream in the first place? When will we trust God enough to allow Him to be our co-pilot, our business partner, our co-author, or whomever we need Him to be in the fulfillment of our God-Sized dream? Whatever it is, there's *nothing* too great for Him…*absolutely nothing*!

> "Behold, I am the Lord, the God of all flesh;
> is there anything too difficult for Me?"
> -Jeremiah 32:27 (NKJV)

Saying "Yes" was not the answer

Saying "Yes" to my God-Sized dream was the best decision I could have ever made, uncertainty and all. However, when I look back, the uncertainty only represented my lack of faith because God was certain all along. It was a moment filled with excitement, nervousness, and lots of questions. I am sure that it is pretty similar to what you felt about pursuing your own dreams or even feel now. I just knew that because I had finally said "yes" after so many years, that God and I were going to be on the fast-track to success. I mean, I had finally given Him the one thing He had been chasing me for, a resounding "yes." But what I didn't realize was that success would take longer than I anticipated. The days, months, and years that followed in my journey did not meet the expectations and timeline of success I eagerly anticipated when I made the decision. Imagine after having a vision of speaking and motivating crowds, to sitting on the sidelines of doing something I thought was impossible, to finally saying "yes" and things not working out as I planned. I just knew that years of fear-filled thoughts and trepidation would finally set off a whirlwind of major wins and successes. Early on, I never once thought that my road to entrepreneurship would be a little bumpy, OK, a lot bumpier, in reality.

Of course, I've heard sayings like, "It takes ten years to make an overnight success" or the advice of "fake it til you make it." I guess I thought *my* "yes" would be different. *My* "yes," would come with a lot more ease and even more rapid growth. I mean why not? It wasn't just a dream. It was *my* calling, the thing I was supposed to do. Surely, I was supposed to walk right into it, or so I thought.

Instead of overnight success, I found a beautiful journey of God's grace, provision, perfect timing, and preparation. I also found the type of relationship I always wanted with my Heavenly Father. One that was consistent. One where I communicated with Him and prayed to Him often. One that included times of fasting and intimate worship where I took everything and laid it at His feet. At least that is how I describe the process of my dream journey now. Prior to the realization of what God was really doing in my life, all I could see, and feel, was delay, discouragement, feeling misunderstood, and loneliness. This does not even include the times where I felt like I was under financial distress.

I am pretty sure the moments you had, or are having, felt similar at certain points. More like, "God, where are you?" versus seeing the visual from the "Footprints in the Sand" poem. You know, the classic spiritual poem where it shows one set of footprints in the sand because Jesus was carrying you during your most difficult season. I found myself in those seasons more often filled with tears, arms flailing, and anxiety. It wasn't until I stopped trying to understand things naturally or make things happen in *my* timing that I began to see that God had not left me. In fact, He had been with me the entire time. He *was* the one who was carrying me. I just had to remember to be the one to cast my cares on Him.

- He was with me when my bank account had zero dollars and nothing I did to generate revenue worked. Until He stepped in and blessed me with $30k worth of business within forty-eight hours.
- He was with me when one year I looked at my Fall schedule and it was completely empty. Then I received a phone call one morning immediately after I finished praying, and the caller said, "I have $15k in my budget and I need your help with something, are you available?"
- He was with me during my first book launch party and one of my corporate clients said, "As long as I have money, you have money!"

Whether it was rejection after rejection or simply hearing crickets, I began to see that every hard moment was actually *the* best moment for me to experience God in a new way. What those moments did was create room for me to get out of the way with all my efforts of striving and allow Him to show up bigger than I imagined in ways and moments I will never forget. I realized He wanted my commitment to Him and the process, not just my "yes." He wanted to be the one who fulfilled my God-Sized dream, not me.

Pursuing your God-Sized dream, for some, may come with ease. But for many, it comes with two very important things:

1. Preparation
2. Process

The key is not to mistake your seasons of preparation and process with what may feel like you misheard God. Just because something is not going as you planned, taking longer than you thought, or is more difficult than you anticipated, it does not mean that God has abandoned you. It may very well mean that *He* is preparing you. It may also mean there is a process to what He wants to do in your life.

Sometimes we begin to subscribe to the things we hear other people say like "Well maybe it's just not my season." But just like my good friend and colleague, Jade Simmons, author of *Audacious Prayers for World Changers,* says,

"It's always your season!"

Jade teaches that it is always your season, you just have to know what season you are in. She explains the importance of knowing your season in order to shift your thinking. Could you be in a season of planting seeds and just starting? Of course, but that doesn't mean it's not your season! Because we live in a technologically advanced, social media highlight-reel driven society, we try to cause our seasons of harvest to come quicker than His plan for that moment. I mean everyone else is living their best life, right? Why shouldn't you?

I will never forget hearing a message from Joyce Meyer, a well-known women's minister and Bible teacher. She was preaching at my church where she recounted the story of her journey. She shared how she vividly remembered when God called her to go and preach the gospel. Just like you and I thought with our own journeys, she thought that meant at that very moment. But no, she said for the next five years she led a Bible study in her home where the same twenty people showed up every week. And on good weeks it would be twenty-five people. She did the set-up, break down and clean up. God's Word was true. She was about to embark upon an international ministry, host international conferences, and write over one-hundred books. It just wasn't all meant to happen at *that* moment.

Like most of us, Joyce Meyer, and so many other influencers we follow, all had to go through a process and season of preparation. The question to consider is will you be consistent? What if Joyce had given up in years three or four and said, "this is taking too long?" What if she said, "I'm not hosting Bible study for these twenty people anymore?" It was her season to teach Bible study in her home to twenty people, just as much as it was her season to embark upon teaching 20,000 or more in arenas all over the world.

Stories like Joyce's always make me think about the void in women's gospel if she had given up. I remember reaching year five in my own journey and feeling so comforted by her story. Without the transformation God did in my own heart by showing me I was on a beautiful journey with Him and stories like Joyce Meyer's, I would have been so discouraged. That's because year five looked nothing like I anticipated. At least not initially. Instead, it looked even better because I was able to understand and see God at work in my life, versus if my growth and success happened overnight.

Think about all of the women who would miss out on the fruits of your dream journey if you never started or if you quit before it was your harvest season? *Her God-Sized Dream* was written to help you:

- See the beauty of your journey and how God desires to bless you along the way.
- See that you are not alone. Many of us have shared the same moments of discouragement as you, only to realize God was with us all along.
- Learn how to overcome the things getting in your way. There is a whole world waiting on your gifts, you can't stop now.
- Increase your faith to go after the dreams God has placed in your heart with everything you have.
- Introduce you to some amazing friends and clients whose beautiful journeys I am sure you can relate to.

Who is this book for?

This book is for the one who knows there is something more to life and more to their career. It is for those who have…

- Been thinking, planning, and researching their dreams.
- Started and taken a few stumbles along the way.
- Become discouraged with the process they've had to go through.
- Reached a few big milestones, but are asking themselves, "Now what? I know there has to be more."

In this book, you will find stories of amazing women who have similar journeys that touch all of us. Some journeys have taken longer than they thought and have been filled with more moments of discouragement than they probably anticipated. But in spite of challenges and delays, they wrote books, launched businesses, and grew their initial dreams into what they now call their God-Sized dream. Each chapter is not only filled with encouraging stories, but also prayers for your own journey, practical questions to help you refocus, and journal space to reflect. This dream-tool offers the perfect combination of initiatives, not just to inspire you, but to elevate you to another level of commitment to your purpose. It will be the fuel for your drive.

Dear God-Sized Dreamer,

Now is not the time for you to stop, stall, or second guess yourself. It is time for you to remember the things God told and promised you. It is time for you to remember you were placed into this world to make a big impact, not just to live a mundane and routine life. You are here to use your gifts for His glory. It's time to change people's lives with your talents, solutions, presence, and voice. The market is not saturated. In fact, it's waiting for you. I know there have been things that have gotten in your way in the past or even right now as you read this, but timing is everything. Maybe you've started and stopped countless times. Maybe you're frustrated because you have been consistent but the results seem very little. But in this season, I encourage you to etch deep in your hearts Galatians 6:9 where it says, "Let us not become weary in doing good, for at the proper time we will reap a harvest if we do not give up." (NIV)

If not you, then who?

One of my favorite stories in the Bible is the story of Esther. She had a very important role to play for an entire nation and generation. Specifically, the scripture says,

"For if you remain silent at this time,
relief and deliverance for the Jews will arise from another place,
but you and your father's family will perish.
And who knows but that you have come to your royal position
for such a time as this?"
Esther 4:14 (NIV)

Esther had an opportunity to remain silent. Just as you have an opportunity to stay where you are and not take another step. Yet there was an entire generation of Jews waiting on relief and deliverance from Esther's courage and obedience. Just because you can't physically see the generation of people who are waiting for you to bring them relief and deliverance, does not mean they are not there. It does not mean they are not waiting on *you* either. Like Esther was told, if she remained silent, relief and deliverance will arise from another place, and it will be the same with you. If you don't act now, someone else will. The areas you are gifted in are needed in this world … your message, book, business, album…it's *all* needed. God cares just as much about the people who need it as He does you. He will use whoever is willing to undergo the preparation and the process to fulfill a specific purpose in the world. If Esther opted out of her chance, someone else would have been chosen. A position I don't want you or I to be in. You are the chosen one and you can no longer remain silent.

…It is for such a time as this!

Chapter 1

7 Steps to Your
God-Sized Dream

Don't hide your idea

There is a story in Matthew 25: 14 - 30, called "The Parable of the Talents." It recaps a conversation a man had with his three servant's aka business besties before he went to Bali (Melissa's version). During that conversation, he entrusted each of them with money. One servant received five bags of gold and silver, another one received two bags, and the last servant received one bag, based on their abilities. By the time the man came back, each of them shared what they did with the money he had entrusted to them. The servant with five bags invested it and made five times more. The next servant invested his as well and made two times more. The last servant, was afraid to lose it so he went and hid it.

The question is which servant are you? I believe you are reading this book because God has given you great ideas. Maybe you are like the first servant and He has given you five ideas. Maybe you are like the second servant and He has given you two. But the question is, even if you are like the third, and He has given you just one, what will you do with it?

Will you be like the first two servants when God checks in on what you've done with the amazing ideas He gave you? Will He find that you invested your time, money, and energy wisely to bring your God-Sized dreams to life? Or will you be like the third servant, afraid, only able to give Him back the idea He originally gave you in the first place?

I cannot emphasize the point enough, and that is, "If you won't do it, someone else will," Matthew 25: 28 - 29 (NLT).

"Then he ordered, 'Take the money from this servant, and give it to the one with the ten bags of silver. *To those who use well what they are given, even more will be given, and they will have an abundance.* But from those who do nothing, even what little they have will be taken away.'"

I already know because you are reading this book, while you may have fear, you are not one of those do-nothing servants. Even in spite of fear, you are a person who takes active steps to make things happen. Even if it's been years since God gave you the idea, you are a finisher. You are going to follow through to hear,

> Well done, good and faithful servant!
> You have been faithful with a few things;
> I will put you in charge of many things.
> Matthew 25: 21 (NIV)

Aunt Gale

In 2016, during a tour for my first book, *The Courageous Life - How to Leap from Your Career to Your Calling,* I met Aunt Gale. She was the aunt of one of my college best friends. She was retiring that year and her sister thought it would be a great event for the two of them to do together. During the book tour stop, I shared the saying of the late Dr. Myles Munroe who often said, "the wealthiest place on earth is the cemetery." I then asked the audience,

"Will you die with your dreams?"

As Aunt Gale thought about her retirement fast approaching in a few months and her lifelong love for baking, she immediately said she didn't want to take her dream of owning a baking business to the grave. Not only did she get to work immediately, but she also started making money quickly.

During the course of writing this book, Aunt Gale sent me a few texts that said,

"The cemetery example you used about businesses that never occurred because they were buried impacted me so much. I asked God to tell me what He would have me to do after retirement in October. I clearly heard cupcakes; make good tasting economical cupcakes. At your event, I wrote I wanted to have a cake business, but God said cupcakes. I had never made cupcakes other than Jiffy corn muffins. I always made sheet cakes, pound cakes & layer cakes during special events & holidays but never a cupcake! As a result of stepping out on faith, my business has grown through word of mouth. My business is done out of my home and my husband is my delivery man. We have our tax and business information set up legally and provide cupcakes for all events like birthdays, anniversaries, baby showers, and more."

If Aunt Gale never started, she would have been just like the third servant who went and hid their talent instead of investing in it. God took her lifelong hobby of baking and gave her a specific strategy ... cupcakes. The length of time it has taken you to start your own dream is not the issue, just don't take it to the cemetery.

Write the vision and make it plain

Before we get into all the things that delay or distract us in our dreams, I want you to pause and give yourself permission to dream for a few moments. Dream just like we used to do when we were kids and felt like we could do anything, be anything, and go anywhere. For most of us, when we were kids anything seemed possible, right? But somewhere between our childlike thoughts full of freedom, we entered into this space called *life* full of everything but freedom. We became consumed with life's pressures like perfection, bills, what will people think, and raising our kids. Many of us also add our self-imposed constraints where we tell ourselves "No!" before anyone else has a chance to. Even if we don't say the actual word "no," it has the same effect when we say things like:

- Who am I to do that?
- I am not qualified to do that!
- Who would read it?
- Who would follow me?
- Who would watch me?
- Who would buy from me?
- I would, but I'm not ready!
- I would, but I have to wait because ________________.

All of these questions and statements are a variation of saying, "No" to your God-Sized dream without using the word "No." Pause for a moment. I want you to say, *"Yes"* and dream for a few moments with no rebuttals and no hesitation. I want you to write down all the things you would love to do if there were no constraints. Nothing is off limits. You will be tempted to not write something down because your mind or your fears will present an impossible constraint. Things like, I would open a restaurant but I work a full-time job that I need or I have a lot of debt. Or I would do "x" but I need to make sure I get my kids through school so I will list something else. For a moment, get rid of your debt, know that your family will be fine, and dream that you have all the time, money, resources, and support in the world.

Write your dream(s) below:

There is only one rule in this exercise and that is to remove the limitations. For these few moments, there are none. You can write. You can draw. Do whatever makes you feel the most creative. Also, don't just share one dream. Share all of them. What is your dream for your marriage/relationship? If you're single, describe your future mate and what your wedding looks like. If you're married, describe your communication, intimacy, and dream vacations. What are your dreams for your kids? What are your dreams for your finances? What is your dream business? You name it, I want you to dream about it. Use the next couple of blank pages to write or draw your dreams.

"Write down the revelation and make it plain on tablets…"
Habakkuk 2:2 (NIV)

My dream is…

____

____

____

____

____

____

____

____

____

____

____

____

____

____

____

____

____

____

7 steps to your God-sized dream

Now that you have written/or drawn your dream(s), let's talk about how to make them a reality. The dream phase is great, but it is the first step. As you read earlier, we need to do a lot more of it as well as exercising our childlike innocence and tendencies. But achieving our dreams does not just happen. As you and I both know, it takes work. And that is why you hear so many stories of people looking back on their lives and telling stories about things they wish they had done or started years ago. However, that will not be your testimony even if your dream is something you should have started in the past. We're not looking back. We're not holding onto guilt. We are only moving forward. Right?

Prerequisite: Surrender
The one prayer you should always say for any dream is, "not my will, but your will be done." This prayer stated with sincerity allows us to yield to our plan and embrace God's plans, timing, and ways versus our own. It also gives us the desire for His best outcome instead of preconceived ideas. But surrendering and saying this prayer is not just for the beginning of your dream, it is for every part of your dream. Before you move on too quickly, know that surrender is not just some quick simple prayer, it is a daily process. It's a daily heart check to say, "God, you are more important than any dream I could ever have. What you want for me is far more than I could ever want for myself." Daily surrender allows you to:

- Trust the process
- Hear God clearly
- Walk and work in peace

Step 1: Map out your dream

The first thing most people say when they talk about what they would like to do most is, "I don't know how?" and then they stop. Step one is where most dreams die simply because most people focus on the end result versus the first step. And if you are like me, you are a *big* dreamer and can look all the way the end and say, "I have no clue how to make that happen."But guess what, you do know how to make it happen. You may not know every step, every process, but you know the first step.

For example, many first-time authors will say, "I don't know how to publish a book."No, you may not. But you do know that publishing a book requires writing a book. Take the first step and start to write while you research the publishing process.

Write out 3 - 5 big milestones that need to happen in order to achieve your dream:

1. ____
____

2. ____
____

3. ____
____

4. ____
____

5. ____
____

Step 2: Start

In order not to let your dreams die in the dream phase, you have to push the start button. Whether you are just starting or leveling up, the action that will give you the most momentum is starting; not thinking, not planning, not talking about it, but starting. I don't know about you but "someday" never came for me. I actually had to take a deep breath and pick a day...with fears, nervous excitement, and all.

What is your dream start date or important next step date?

____

Step 3: Create a routine

The top two things we always complain about are our time and our energy. Either we don't have enough time or when we do, we are too tired. Once you hit the start button the number one thing to help you keep momentum is going to be routine. What are the days and times in your schedule you can commit to follow-through on your, "Yes?"

Write a sample routine below:

____

____

____

____

____

Step 4: Get Support

The great thing about this journey is that it is not meant for you to take alone. It comes with support, not only the support of your friends, families, and mentors but others within your reach. This can include those you hire or those who have gone before you to help show you the how-to's and help you with follow-through and accountability. Write a list of those who are or will be on your dream support team.

1. _______________________________________

2. _______________________________________

3. _______________________________________

4. _______________________________________

5. _______________________________________

Step 5: Motivation Mastery

The #1 thing you will have to master during the pursuit of your God-Sized dream is your faith. The excitement of starting, or even your wins, will only last but so long. You will need to have your "go to" resources for daily motivation. Your faith will be tested. It could be tested with things such as the length of time it takes to complete, the hours you have to put in each week, life challenges, and more. Or it could be tested because of your lack of confidence and self-doubt. If you are constantly battling thoughts such as, "I could never do this," then how will you deal with it? Will it be through prayer, listening to your favorite motivational speakers, meditation, or podcasts?

Whatever your source of motivation, you will need plenty of it to endure the highs and lows that come along with pursuing your dream.

How do you or will you keep yourself motivated? Be specific.

____

____

____

Step 6: Celebrate Wins and Milestones

Every win counts. The day you map out your dreams counts. The day you start counts. The day you get that special email counts. The days someone says yes counts, whether it is the 1st or the 50th time. It all counts. The problem is we often discount it. We frown our nose at times because we are at the beginning and not the end. Or we're in the middle and not the end. Or it didn't turn out like we wanted, even though it was the first time we took this step. Whatever it is, make sure you pause to celebrate your wins, no matter how big or small. It will be much-needed fuel for the rest of the journey.

How do you or will you celebrate your wins and milestones? And before you say, "I don't typically celebrate," what would it be if you did?

____

____

____

Step 7. Repeat

Start the process all over again. Know that your dream is absolutely achievable. It's achievable because your dream map is broken down into big milestones and daily activities. Once you hit a milestone, go back up to step one, update your dream map and hit the start button on the next thing, and repeat. The fastest way to your dream is in motion, not in your thoughts!

Chapter 2

Five Things Getting in the Way of Your God-Sized Dream

Wait, did you do the dream exercise? If not go back and do it. Don't skip the process. It's our lack of willingness to take the time to dream that keeps us repeating yesterday's cycles.

5 Phases of a Dream

Now that you completed the dream exercise, heard Aunt Gale's amazing testimony, and know for a fact you are not going to be like the fearful servant number three, let's discuss the five phases of a dream. If you like to garden, then this analogy will be familiar to you.

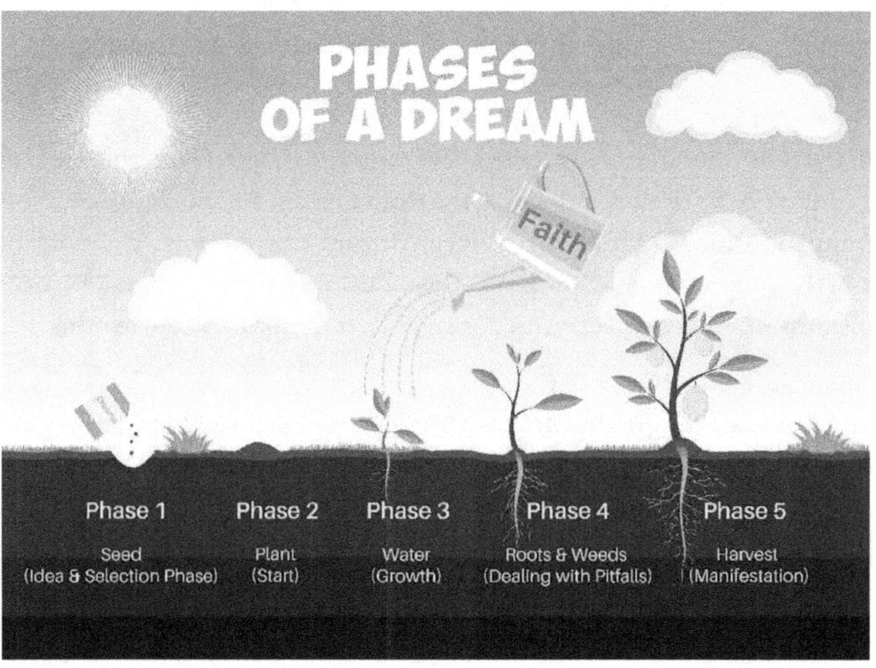

Phase 1: Seed (Idea & Selection Phase)

This is the phase where you know there is something more for you to do. It is where you choose the dream and start to move. It might sound crazy, you might not even know how to do it, you just have this inkling you should take action. For some people, it may be one specific thing, such as, "I want to go back to school, I want to open a salon, or I want to write a book." For others, you have several ideas, all of which are viable. Whether you have one great idea or several to choose from, this is the phase where you select which God-Sized idea you will pursue.

For those who have more than one great idea, don't get stuck on which one is the best. While a coach or mentor can help you prioritize, it could be that they are all good. Lysa Terkeurst talks about the power to choose what we want to do in life, in her book, *The Best Yes*. She reminds of Isaiah 30:21 that says, "Whether you turn to the right or to the left, your ears will hear a voice behind you, saying, 'This is the way; walk in it.'"

Phase 2: Plant (Start)

Phase 2 is the start-up process. It's where we go from thinking to committing to action. It's also the foundation for the journey. The foundation looks different for every dream. For authors, it would be your book outline and proposal. For business owners, it might be a business or strategy plan. And for singers, it might be voice lessons.

Phase 3: Water (Growth)

No seed has ever grown without water and nutrients, which means *your dream* will not grow without water and nutrients. This is where you are not only working on your dream but investing in yourself and your God-Sized idea. You are diligently working towards achieving your milestones *and* working on getting better at your craft. This could look like going to an industry conference, reading related books and articles, or investing in courses and coaching to help you grow.

Phase 4: Weed (Dealing with Pitfalls)

Most gardens I come across have had a weed problem at some point in time. They can be a pest to the most beautiful gardens and take a lot of work to prevent and/or get rid of them. Every dreamer has to deal with pitfalls of rejection, disappointment, and overcoming failure. None of which mean you will not be able to achieve your dream. Just like weeds can be expected in the gardening process, so can these minor setbacks. Even the best gardener with the most preventive methods will walk outside one day and see a weed. It's inevitable, just as the pitfalls of every dreamer's journey. It doesn't mean that it will not work and it definitely does not mean you should quit.

Phase 5: Harvest (Manifestation)

Gardeners have two best days: the day they go out and see the first sighting of whatever they planted and the day they go out and see it in full bloom. Both days and the journey in-between are all worth celebrating. The thing about the first and the last day is that it can feel like forever. It can seem like an eternity from the time the seed was planted and when it begins to show the first sign of life. Time can appear endless before that first sign of life is in full bloom and then one day you walk outside and wonder, when did that happen?

Your dream will be just like that. Full of days that seem longer than you anticipated, wondering when is it going to happen? And filled with moments and milestones wondering, wow, when did that happen?

Share below what phase you are in? Describe in detail.

____

____

____

____

____

But first, you must say, "Yes!"

But before you can say, "wow, when did that happen?" You have to say, "Yes, God, I'll do it." For most people, it's not a quick yes. At least it wasn't for me.

Why did it take me so many years to finally say "yes" to my God-Sized dream? The answer is both simple and complex. It's even harder to articulate to someone else to understand unless you've been there. I can say the short four or five-letter words like fear, doubt, and trust were the culprits, but the truth is, each one of those dream-killing behaviors could be a book all to itself.

There is a myriad of reasons why people stop short of pursuing their God-Sized dreams. I watch people like myself, my clients, and those that I follow, do it every day. The biggest highlight of my day is watching someone go from thinking about the things in their heart to resolving within themselves and their relationship with God to *go for it*. I see that same excitement and nervousness in them that was in me, when I ultimately said "yes." They finally see the confidence needed to start taking active steps towards making it happen. They are no longer as intimidated by the process (at least what they know of it) or the outcome.

However, their "yes," is just the beginning. I have watched the women who share their stories in *Her God-Sized Dream* keep going in spite of. You will be amazed at how each one kept going in spite of:

- Their Age
- How small they had to start
- Distractions that tried to take them out
- Working a full-time job
- What their finances looked like

These are five of the most common things that get in people's way when they are pursuing their God-Sized dream. It causes some not to start, most to stall at certain junctures, and others to quit altogether. So, I wanted to share with you the journeys of five amazing women just like yourself who are:

- Pursuing Her Dream at Any Age
- Not Despising Small Beginnings
- Overcoming Distractions
- Pursuing Her Dream While Working a 9-to-5
- Preparing Her Faith and Finances

There are even more things we can list such as pursuing your dream while raising children or dealing with an unsupportive spouse. No matter what your obstacle, know that it is absolutely normal to deal with and even wrestle with any one of these. For many people, it's more than one. For the woman who is struggling in her faith, working full-time, raising children, dealing with negative thinking, and your resources seem to be limited...*do...not...give...up*. This book is definitely for you.

Achieving your dream at any age

Somehow, we bought into this notion that pursuing our dreams should only happen during certain time periods in our lives. Time periods such as in your early 20s before you get married and have kids. That's because everyone says once you have kids, you have to wait until you are an empty nester to live out your dreams...but by that point, you need to wait until you are fully retired because it would be careless to leave your career now after all these years with so much vested. In the past, when people were considered too young to start a business, we now have more millennial entrepreneurs than ever before.

Some of you might say, "Who do I think I am starting over at this age, trying something new, writing, speaking or launching a business?" How dare you try to become anything other than the labels and titles either society, your family, or the ones you have assigned to yourself. Who do you think you are to finally come to the realization that it is never too late for God to use you? Have you not heard that the best things happen as you mature in age? Since the older you get, the wiser you are; Now is not the time for you to slow down, take a back seat, or give up on your God-Sized dream. Instead, it's time for you to begin to ask God to use you like He did Sarah when she gave birth at the age of ninety and Abraham was one-hundred years old. I don't know what age you are, but I do know that there's no limit on what God can do in your life.

We walk around subjecting ourselves and others to the mindset of it's either too early in our life, we don't know enough, we missed our moment, or it's just not the right time. Why? Because to do anything other than work full-time at the same job for forty years would be careless and irresponsible. The truth is, there will *never* be a perfect time. There will always be something vying for your attention or seem even more important than walking in full obedience to the things God has called you to do. I can't wait for you to read about Joan's story of how she decided to pursue her own dreams and reinvent her life in her late 50s.

Don't despise small beginnings

Raise your hand if you have ever stopped yourself from starting or continuing something because it was not going to look like someone else's journey. I am a firm believer that comparison is the biggest killer of most people's dreams. We get jealous and downright discouraged viewing other people's social media highlight reel that's not even *real*. Watching other people will always make it seem like they are going faster and further than you. It starts to diminish and dishonor the amazing courageous steps you have already taken. These thoughts only leave you feeling like you are not making progress and moving backward, in the wrong direction.

Every person of influence you follow had two things: a day one and some sort of mountain to climb that they had to overcome. Yes, maybe a *few* had quick journeys. But many have had journeys like you and me.

Days/Moments that started off smaller than we anticipated and took longer than we ever thought. Before there was a megachurch called the Potter's House in Dallas, Texas led by Bishop T.D. Jakes, there was an unknown pastor in a small church in West Virginia. Before there was a global movement of Elevation Church led by Pastor Steven Furtick, there were his first few years of ministry where he preached to the same ten families. Get ready for Lana Hunter's story of hosting the Sundress & Big Hat Brunch in her church for years, before becoming a multi-city, international women's event that it is today. Lana's story will inspire you.

Overcoming distractions

Have you ever had one of those, "if it's not one thing, it's another" type moments? We all have had those instances where we set out to do something and one thing comes up after another. They are called distractions.

In its simplest form, distractions look and feel like a phone call you need to take as soon as you get settled and focused on your project. Or an impromptu errand that needs to be handled immediately. Followed by an urgent need and prayer request from a close girlfriend that you can't ignore, so you drop everything for the next hour.

In its largest form, distractions can be in your health or the health of someone close to you, or even your finances. Almost to the point where you feel like it is a spiritual attack that every time you try to make progress on the things God has called you to do something major happens in the lives of your children, your marriage, or some other important area of your life.

Big or small, or even things unheard of, they are the things that cause you to say, "I would be further along…BUT!"
- I would be further along but work is so busy
- I would be further along but my family demands so much of my attention

- I would be further along but my husband says we need to spend more time together
- I would be further along but there is just so much to do around the house when I get home from work that I can't keep up

In reality, work, your family, your spouse, and so many other things *are not* distractions in and of themselves. They only become distractions when:

1. You *know* you have a God-sized dream you should be pursuing

2. You never create the space or make the sacrifice to pursue it

What is your BUT? What are the things that are eating away at your time, energy, or even your health? Even in an ideal world, there is never enough time to do it all. But when we are called to do something, we are also given the grace to do it.

Distractions do not have to be a deterrent to your destiny. The biggest mistake we make is taking the pursuit of our God-Sized dreams too lightly. We have this naïve assumption that it will be easy. The reason why it's so hard to write the book is because the enemy's number one job is to:

> ...Steal and kill and destroy
> - John 10:10 NIV

He comes to steal your dreams. Kill your motivation. Destroy your faith so you believe it won't ever happen. The distractions come and cause you to either: 1) not start or 2) not finish. But the other half of that verse states, "I have come that they may have life and they have it more abundantly" (NKJV). In order to not live in regret and walk in that level of abundance, we must take the pursuit of our dreams seriously. Which means, if you keep dealing with the same distractions over and over, what are you willing to change? How fervently are you willing to pray? How long are you willing to fast? How often are you willing to spend quality time with God outside of your routine devotional time on the way to work? We have to be willing to do whatever it takes to overcome the things that distract us from our dreams. Otherwise, we will keep going around the same mountains until it becomes a familiar route we are comfortable with and it ultimately destroys our destiny.

Cheryl's story of overcoming day-to-day and spiritual distractions will inspire you to move past the nagging delays getting in your own way.

Pursuing your dream while working your 9-to-5

Have you ever felt like quitting your day job to pursue your dream job? Yes, me too and I did! But then I retracted my two-week notice after I realized I was full of passion but had no profitable business plan. People get excited listening to the overnight success stories of online marketers or motivational speakers. We get so attracted to the outcome, but we are not willing to pay the price and amount of sacrifices they have paid. Every time I meet someone who gets excited about my story or the message of *The Courageous Life – How to Leap from Your Career to Your Calling,* I quickly hit the pause button. I tell them how we get so enamored with what we see in others, falsely thinking that if we just take that leap and do the work the same thing will happen for us.

While I wish it were that simple, it's not. In a nutshell, taking a leap is what you have to do, but everyone's process is different. Your process may take you less than twelve months, where someone else's journey may take them over ten years. This is why I encourage others to start and build while they are employed, unless you *know* for sure that God has told you to leave. But building your dream while you work is complicated and takes discipline. Just because you finally said "yes" does not mean all of your other responsibilities at work, your family, in your community or at church are on board with your "yes."

It takes discipline. The reason why I was ready to leap from my career to my calling - was because I had been working on my dream while with my employer. The reason why others are able to have multiple streams of income without depleting their savings or 401k is because they start to build while they work. The thing you will have to figure out is what will it take for you to start? How will you manage your time? How will you manage your priorities?

Kimberly's story of how she launched her dream as an executive with a hectic international travel schedule and other major commitments will leave you rejuvenated and ready to refocus.

Preparing your faith and finances

I mentioned earlier that pursuing your God-Sized dream often requires two things 1) preparation and 2) process. But the preparation comes in multiple facets. The first one is the type of preparation that God does in you before you reach various milestones of success or enter into certain seasons. The other is the type of preparation *you* yourself know how to do. This preparation is when you begin to own your dream and transition from thinking to planning. The two areas you can prepare most whether it is before you start your God-Sized dream or during, are your faith and your finances.

When I finally started my coaching and training company, I was so proud of *my*, "Yes!" I felt like I had finally found enough faith to trust God to pursue my dreams. That "yes" meant everything to me. You will often hear people say, "All it takes is one 'yes'". And while it's true, they forget the other critical parts of the story. The parts about the preparation and the process. The parts where you will have to say "yes" again and again every time you encounter difficulty. I felt like every single door that was ever placed in front of me was going to magically open up as soon as I presented myself. How naïve of me!

The reason why I talk so much about courage is because I know that courage and faith are the things needed every single morning when I wake up. Most of the time, I'm looking at God saying, "What's next? How do we do this? Where do we go from here?" I didn't realize that I would be faced with having to overcome that same barrier to my faith and trusting God many times over after that initial day. I didn't realize that my faith trials of trusting God to be my provider, to supply the next client, to rest in Him, would be the thing that I would battle most, day after day. I was definitely mistaken.

Many times, trusting God requires a level of prayer and tears that most people do not understand. Your journey will not resemble the highlight reel of your favorite social media influencers. Instead, it will resemble whatever process God has to take *you* through to be able to handle what's coming next. If I had to look back and give advice to my younger self and to you, it would be to prepare your faith…continuously. Each new milestone, level of elevation, and turn in your journey will require a fresh perspective on faith and a new revelation of who God is to you *today*. Sometimes that will look like you remembering who He has been and what He has done for you in the past. Other times, it will look like understanding who He is and what the Word says about Him and your life in a new way. Either way, preparing and renewing your faith are essential.

The other area vital for preparation is your finances. It's funny how we will pray for six and seven-figure businesses, best-selling books and more, but we are not good stewards of our own personal finances. If you don't pay your personal bills on time what makes you think you will pay your business bills on time? If you are not good at saving now, how will you save and invest in your business in the future? In addition, for those that long to be full-time entrepreneurs, how are you preparing to handle the transition of getting paid every other week to generating your own revenue, especially in the business building stage? The worst time to learn is during the journey, the best time to learn and prepare is *before* you start.

Nyisha's story of how she prepared her faith and finances for her God-Sized dream will cause you to reevaluate how you need to prepare for your own God-Sized dream.

What's your dream?

The stories that follow are from amazing women just like you. Each of them has relatable experiences and faced the same type of distractions you've probably faced. What I love about their stories is how they overcame their obstacles and continuously overcome them to start, launch, and work on their God-Sized dream. Many are somewhere in between the beginning and middle of their journeys walking by faith, trusting God, and being relentless about not settling beneath their purpose.

Pursuing your God-Sized dream will more than likely be one of the hardest things you have ever done. But my prayer for you is that you begin to realize that your journey is not about the outcome of your dream at all, but it was always about your relationship with Him. More importantly, I hope that you see the beauty each woman found in the One who gave them their dream in the first place.

As you read their stories, I pray that you give God back all of the things that have been getting in your way: Your doubts, your fears, your questions, your anxiety, and your mistakes. Whatever you were dealing with when you picked up this book, God can handle. You will not be the person that gives up on their dreams. Instead, you will learn to trust God like never before. You will walk in crazy levels of faith and favor. And you will begin to see change and transformation in your thinking and the development of your ideas.

Hold on, you *will* achieve your God-Sized dream.

Chapter 3

Don't Despise Small Beginnings

Lana Hunter

"Before I formed you in the womb I knew you,
before you were born I set you apart;
I appointed you as a prophet to the nations."
Jeremiah 1:5 (NIV)

My name was chosen long before I was born. My mother's favorite actress at the time was Lana Turner. And even though she had four boys, she'd said, "If I ever have a girl her name will be Lana." So I'm Lana.

Two years after my brother Dale, I came along. I would be the only girl my mother would have. After me, there were two other bighead little boys. I am a firm believer that names matter, have power, and should not be given lightly. You are speaking into a child's future with the name you give them. I happen to love my name and can't imagine having any other name. In Hawaiian it means "buoyant, to float"; that's the ability to come back, survive and float. In Irish, it means "little rock," strong and resilient. I am honored that God knew this is who I would be. Therefore, who am I to be anything less than whom God called me to be?

I always say, "I'm Bahamian by birth and American by choice." However, my Caribbean birth and influences make me very proud and colorful. I called the Bahamas home until age nine, and then my family moved to Miami, Florida. Education and opportunity were always important to my now deceased father. He wanted his children to be in a country that afforded them the most opportunities. For him, that was America. Even though I was leaving everything I had known, I was excited about "coming to the states." I had no frame of reference, but the thought of someplace new excited me to no end. Still today, the unknown excites me.

I would call Miami home for the next sixteen years. I love Miami. It is a melting pot of people, cultures, and languages. Hearing five different dialects spoken in your neighborhood today might be familiar. However, in the early '80s, it was fascinating! I learned so many different cultures and saw how everyone's not the same, but it's okay to be different. I had friends that were black, white, Latin, Jewish, gay-you name it. There was room for everyone and I loved it all.

Having been exposed to "every kind of person," I was ready for my first job right out of high school. I worked for one of the largest trial attorney law firms in downtown Miami. And it was there where my exposure to "all kinds of people" became a valuable asset. I learned that I loved working with people and that I was "good with people." People from all walks of life and various backgrounds. It always seemed that people were naturally drawn to me and enjoyed being around me. So as I started my first job as a working adult, I didn't have any significant career path that I always dreamed of doing. I just knew that I wanted to do enjoyable work with people and not computers or alone in a lab somewhere. So every job since that first job after high school involved actively working with people.

This love of people continued and expanded. I learned that I was good at engaging people. I was also a planner and organizer by nature. Finding any occasion to organize, plan, and host an event was what I thought everyone spent their days thinking about. So whenever there was an event to plan or a fabulous event to execute, I was the go-to person.

I've shared my back story with you to let you know that you don't need to be anyone special, from anywhere particular, or even have a four-year degree. All you need is a God-Sized dream and the work ethic to make that dream a reality. I didn't even know what was about to be birthed in my life. However, who I was and what came naturally to me was about to collide and become my God-Sized dream.

To have a friend, you must first be a friend.

I moved to North Carolina in my mid-twenties. During that time, event planning quickly became what I was known for. Since like minds are attracted to each other, I quickly found my circle. From baby showers, bridal showers, ladies' brunches, anniversary parties, you name it, my friends and I did it. So it was with this group of friends that nurtured and gave birth to what would become the Sundress & Big Hat Brunch™.

One day over brunch with a circle of girlfriends I asked "What happened to those old-fashioned tea parties our grandmothers dragged us to? At first, everyone was like, "What? What do you mean?" I said "You remember those Rainbow Teas with cucumber sandwiches and tea cakes? Did you all forget about those hats, lace gloves, and a church lady suit!" We all laughed because everyone had a mental picture of those suits. However, then I got to thinking," why not?" Why not bring them back? Just more our style and with our flair. I'm a firm believer in "Don't talk about it, be about it!" And guess what? My friends were crazy enough to say "yes" to this silly idea. We never imagined that this thought would become a thing and that thing would eventually become my God-Sized dream. This was the birth of the annual "Sundress & Big Hat Brunch™."

I immediately got to work before we all changed our minds. Honestly, the idea got a hold of me, and I couldn't stop thinking about it. The thought of it made me smile and the ideas started flowing. It never seemed like work. I wasn't sure how it would turn out, but I wanted to do it regardless of the outcome. However, what I knew for sure was that I wanted it to be for women, about women, and in support of women.

Also, I knew I wanted to raise money to give to a cause that mattered to us.

With all the excitement, I had no idea what to do or where to start. All I knew for sure was that I had a tribe (aka my girlfriends) willing, able, and ready to support me and my crazy idea. Thank God for a tribe! Everyone needs a tribe. Your tribe might change, evolve, or even shrink, but everyone needs a tribe. So my tribe and I got to planning this thing.

Remember I said we attract who we are? Well, I believe in the law of attraction. I consider myself a creative, so I found there were other creatives around me. I am an event planner and had other event planners around me. My tribe had everything I needed which actually made us a well-rounded tribe. Everyone had a skillset to help carry out this crazy idea. There were even some who said "I can only help you on the day of the brunch and greet people" to which I replied, "Thank You and see you then." I took all the help I could get. I know that it's important to identify who's in your tribe and allow them to help at the level they are willing and able.

So within a few weeks of my crazy idea, we had our first event all scheduled and planned out. We gave ourselves about six months to pull it off. Everyone had their marching orders and was excited and ready in the beginning. As time went on, priorities changed, and life got busy for some. However, my focus never waned. This idea was too deep in me for me to turn back. I'd told too many people that I was doing this thing and the reason I was doing it so it had to go on. This is why it's important to share your dreams. People will hold you accountable which gives you that extra push to keep going.

Well, I made it! Low and behold brunch week finally arrived. I was still trying to convince people to attend. There were about forty people committed but I had prepared for sixty to seventy. So I made more flyers to hand out. I called more friends and asked them to come or if they couldn't make it, tell someone else about it. I reached out to local churches to invite their ladies to attend. I placed ads on local internet radio stations and even did a press release. I was a woman on a mission.

So now it's the day before the inaugural brunch. My husband and resident photographer went to the site to do a lighting check. As he checked in with the receptionist, she politely informed him that "there was no event scheduled for the following day." He stated, "There must be a mistake. My wife has an event here tomorrow, and it has been on the schedule for months. Again, she checked the computer and again responded, "No sir, there is nothing scheduled, and we can't accommodate an event tomorrow." He called me and relayed the whole story to me. I must admit he tried his best to be calm and explained the situation as if it was no big deal to keep me calm.

I was at work and although I was dumbfounded by this news, surprisingly, I wasn't freaked out. My mind kicked into high gear and began to figure out my next move. I told my manager what was going on and to her credit, she said, "Go!" Everyone knew how hard I'd worked on this event and how excited I was about it. I wasn't shouting what I was doing from the mountain tops, but I wasn't making moves in silence either. "What gets talked about gets done." Moreover, I wanted to do the things I said I would do instead of looking and feeling shame when someone asked me about it. I refused to make up an excuse (aka lie) as to why I had not done it.

The issue with the venue was a teaching moment I will never forget. When I began telling people about my crazy idea, I got so much support. One of those early supporters was from a woman who had just launched her first book. She said she'd made great connections with someone that manages this excellent event space. She said it would be perfect for my event and offered to negotiate to get me the space free of charge. And for this, I would allow her to be my speaker and promote her book. It seemed like a win-win to me and so I agreed.

My husband and I went to view the space several times. We even became friendly with the receptionist whom I was trying to convince to come out to the event. However, I never spoke with the event space manager or had *any* communication with her. I trusted someone else to manage that relationship. This was my lesson to learn; when your name is on it, you are entirely responsible for *all* of it. I now look at everything and leave nothing to chance. If a ball gets dropped, then I knew about it, and I was the one who dropped it.

How we were able to pull it all off is still a mystery to me but not to God. He showed up and showed me He was in control as always. On my way from the office, I called my pastor and explained the situation to him. He knew about the event, and thankfully he agreed to let us host the brunch at the church.

After speaking with my pastor, I immediately began calling my tribe from the car. After explaining what happened too many times to count, for the most part, most were able to help out. We had to call the caterers and let them know there was a change in venue. We had to arrange tables and chairs be delivered to the church that afternoon. We had to call some of the men from the church to help with the setup. It was no small feat, but I was determined that we would move forward. And finally, we had to try and reach everyone we knew was coming and advise them of the change of location. There were so many moving parts I have no idea how nothing fell through the cracks.

However, we did it! It is still a miracle that we were able to pull it off. Not only did we do it, but it was a smashing success. From the outside looking in you would have no idea all that had to happen to make this all come together in such short notice. Our first brunch had fifty to fifty-five women. The audience was mostly made up of friends, church members, and co-workers. We laughed, played get to know you games, and created memories that still make me smile thinking about it all. The caterers did a fantastic job. The men from our church served the women dressed like five-star restaurant servers. And everyone wanted to know when we were going to do it again the following year!

I did not start out wanting to host an annual brunch. The plan was just to do it for nostalgia sake and see how it goes. However, after that first brunch, there was an expectation that it would be an annual event. I was thinking "Do you know how hard it was to pull this one off?" Even as I was saying it, I knew God was pressing me to keep going. I somehow knew I had to keep going because it was important to me that women:

- Have a yearly event to look forward to

- Met women outside of their everyday circle

- Have an occasion to get dressed up, laugh a little and share the stories of our lives with other women

- Have an opportunity to be good citizens and raise money to give to those in need

We hosted the brunch at our church for the next three years. However, I never really wanted the brunch to be a "church" event. I tried to reach women that may not go to a church and have a place for them to feel welcomed. I wanted us to reach people that we might not otherwise get to know.

By year four, we graduated and moved to the brand new Hampton Inn & Suites. We had eighty ladies and the tide had shifted. Most were women that were not from the church or friends of mine. Most were invited by someone who had attended in the past or found the event online.

This was also the year life threw me a curveball. I was laid off from my job. My husband and biggest supporter said he didn't want me to go back to work. He knew I was happiest serving others and hosting the brunch. He permitted me to focus on those things, and so I did. This crazy idea was now what my life revolved around anyway, so why not do it full-time? I was always planning, preparing, negotiating ideas, people and venues so this was totally my lane. It was a lot, but I had never been happier. Honestly, it didn't seem like work but what I was really made to do!

It's easy these days to look on social media and see someone who just started hosting events to post a sold-out meme on their timeline. I always thought, *wow, that was easy - for them.* That wasn't my testimony. For me, it was a struggle every year just to fill the room. I practically begged women to come. I passed out flyers and harassed (or should I say threatened) my friends and even strangers to attend. I always made sure my mom and nieces were there to at least fill one table. There were times on the journey when attendance went down from the previous year.

Many other event planners might have become discouraged in the early years. However, I kept getting up and kept doing it because I knew I was walking in my calling. I knew women were waiting for me. Women looked forward to this event every year. They were traveling from other states to attend. We heard stories of women being blessed and encouraged by the brunch. We heard about relationships being restored as a result of something that was shared at the brunch. Mothers and daughters made plans to attend the brunch annually. So how could I stop? How could I allow my pride to get in the way? This thing was bigger than me now and I had to push forward.

Many times, my husband and I had to come out of pocket to cover the expenses. Thankfully, he believed in me, and I believed in what I was doing. So we pushed forward. I've made it a habit to fast and pray for the brunch events, the women who will attend, the venues, the food, and even the activities. I solicit prayers from friends and family. I read about other events and sometimes attend those events to see what we could do better. This thing had become a part of who I am. That's what a God-Sized dream will do.

We had no inkling when I had this crazy idea that this thing would become a real business. After all, it was just for fun, right? I assumed we would sell enough tickets to cover all of the expenses and have some leftovers to give away. Well, that didn't happen. Even God-Sized dreams need funding. Putting on a quality event cost money; a lot of money. I knew I needed to increase ticket prices if we were going to continue. We weren't at the church anymore. There's a significant cost difference in hosting an event at your church and then hosting an event at a country club (which was my goal in the beginning). Those venues wanted their money as soon as the ink dried on the contract and they didn't care that I was doing "God's work."

From the very first brunch, it was my goal to one day host the brunch at a country club. But not just any country club. My goal was to be at the Prestonwood Country Club in Cary, NC. To me, the Prestonwood held a prestige I wanted the brunch to be associated with. The property is immaculate. The views are spectacular and the dark oak wood french doors make you feel like you are living life like it's golden! LOL- at least that's how I felt.

For years I would say, "We will be at Prestonwood soon." I might have been saying it, but the reality seemed so far out of my reach. My abilities and resources were dictating my vision. However, now that I've seen God do more than I could even think or imagine, I dream big! Times have changed and so have I. When you see God do it once, it gets easier to believe He will do it again and again.

We hosted the brunch at the church for the first three years and then at the Hampton Inn & Suites for the next four years. It wasn't until year seven that we sold out at the Hampton Inn with a maximum capacity of 135 women. After that sell-out crowd, my mindset shifted. I finally decided to have enough faith not just to find a larger hotel, but to go after my dream venue.

When I walked into the Prestonwood Country Club in year eight to start the negotiations, it felt like a dream! However, God is so utterly amazing. He had someone in place to act on our behalf. Our point of contact was so accommodating and kind. It was like she had been waiting for us. That's when I knew God was waiting for me to take the first step because He had already gone before me putting everything in order. However, it would take my faith to unlock that door. When I penned that deal, I cried, danced and celebrated like I'd lost my mind. It was terrific, and now I needed to dream bigger. Looking back, we are going into year ten and host events at country clubs and other venues just as lovely, throughout the U.S. and internationally. God is a good God!

So the thing that was a crazy idea while at lunch with girlfriends had now become not only my purpose but my God-Sized dream. Every year we witnessed powerful stories and relationships being restored, started or healed. And all of this was happening at my event. Somehow one year turned into two, then five, and now ten! I often think, "What if I had never started?" What if I allowed my rough start to stop me?" What if I let the years of slow growth discourage me?" When I think that if I had let my crazy dream be just that, then I would not have had the chance to impact *thousands* of women over the last decade.

Shifting the atmosphere

As I mentioned, during the first few years, my tribe slowly begin to shrink as life pulled each of us in different directions. First, one of my close friends and founders, Rochelle Saddler, passed away after battling breast cancer. Talk about hard. I couldn't imagine moving forward without her. I could count on her entirely and deeply for whatever I needed. She was the one who pushed me. She always had great ideas and wasn't afraid of working hard to make this thing happen and grow.

Then other members of the tribe moved away, got married, or changed jobs and couldn't be as involved as they were in the beginning. However, the work still needed to get done. My vision and goal never changed. I knew that it was necessary to continue even if it was just my husband and me. However, when you say "yes" and are walking in the calling and vision God gave you, He also provides and sends you who you need right on time.

My mother always tells me that I have great friends and I must agree (but I'm biased). One of these great friends Kristi introduced me to my now good friend and partner in crime, Melissa. Kristi and I had been friends, more like family for years. She and Melissa grew up together. Melissa and I met the second year of the brunch when Kristi was the speaker. No immediate connection, but God knew. A few years later, we both realized He had planted the seed for the makings of a God connection.

By the time the God connection between Melissa and I occurred, she had recently taken a leap of faith and stepped into her purpose. In her corporate job, she led large-scale initiatives and change. This was her first year on her own, but it was my fifth year. The number five means "grace." Grace is exactly what I needed at the time to continue and Melissa helped me walk into that grace.

I know event planning well. I can decorate the heck out of a space. I can talk to people and make them feel comfortable like we've been friends forever. And there are hosts of other things I can do well. However, what I needed during that fifth year was help seeing the bigger picture. I needed help making some changes to my business model - heck, I needed a business model! I was doing what I knew how to do; host amazing events. As the footprint, impact, and brand of the brunch were growing, I needed more than just hosting skills for this new level and season. So, God connected Melissa and I. We got to work right away. She helped me to see this idea was now a business and had to be run like one. I was hopeful but still a little resistant to change, especially since the impact of the changes weren't immediately evident. It took two more years to see where God was leading us.

The number seven represents "spiritual perfection." Don't get me wrong, by no means does this mean I'd reached some spiritual pinnacle or epiphany. However, it took seven years for the shift to happen for me. I had to learn to show up ready to serve, knowing I was living in, and on purpose year after year, and doing what I was created for.

I see a cloud…

Are you familiar with the story in the Bible where Elijah prayed for rain? (1 Kings 18:41-19:8) There had been no rain for years. After each prayer, he sent his servant out to look for rain. The servant would go out and look, and look, and look. But nothing. Then on the seventh look, the servant said, "I see a cloud..."

It was in my seventh year, after years of begging, harassing, and threatening people to attend the brunch that it finally sold-out. It was three days before the brunch, and we were still getting inquiries for tickets. We literally could not fit another person in the room. We actually had to turn folks away. Yes, turn people away from the same event where in the past, I'd give tickets away to fill the room.

The following year, year eight (the year of new beginnings), we were finally at the Prestonwood Country Club. This was the year we expanded and went to another state! I felt it was time to stop playing it safe; it was time to expand. To my shock and amazement, we sold out two cities two months before the actual event dates. How did this happen? We just grew into my dream venue, filled it with almost two hundred women, and then went to a city where we had no presence or footprint and sold out. Only God could have set this all up!

Enlarge my territory

Let me backup for a minute. A couple of years before year eight, a man (a prophet) I did not know from across the world was a visiting guest speaker at our church. I wasn't even in the room. He called my husband out and asked: "what is this thing your wife is doing with hats?" He said: "Tell her God said to go and do it." I was teaching children's church. My husband was the church photographer and was capturing the service when all of this happened. He couldn't wait (nor could all the other folks at church) to share this news with me. Talk about a God-Sized dream! I was doing what I was doing at the level I was doing it. What did it all mean to "go and do it?" How? When? Where? With what money? I mean, did he know that it took me seven years to sell out in a city where I had friends and family? Now, how am I'm supposed to just "go and do it" where no one knew me? I needed answers, but in reality, I needed to step out on faith.

I wasn't sure what it all meant. However, what I did know for sure was that God was in it and said: "go." Even with that "go" from God, I moved slowly. However, I thank God for covenant connections. Melissa, who had now been helping me, knew what the man of God said. So, in year eight she pushed and said: "Listen, I think it's time to expand." I said what every God-fearing believer says when they are "spiritual, (translation: hiding out in fear) "Let me pray about it." I knew I didn't need to pray about this because I had already been praying and had already heard from God. Fear was trying to keep me "safe" and "comfortable". It was merely a lack of faith.

After I stopped letting fear dictate my faith, I did like Elijah and told the people to prepare for rain! For me, it was taking the brunch on the road to Atlanta. Talk about being nervous. I knew nothing about the Atlanta market. All I knew was that I was supposed to be there. We took a trip to Atlanta and visited several locations that matched the experience we wanted to create. We narrowed our choices down by location, pricing, parking and of course the beauty of the space.

Remember, I didn't know locations, had zero connections, except for one friend in the area, nor did I know if the people even wanted to attend this fancy brunch thing. All I knew was that Atlanta had many celebrities and they do events big in the Peach State all the time. So, I thought, "Will my little brunch make it?" In my mind, I said, "I'll go, but I'll start small." After all, we're supposed to be wise as a serpent, right? It was just me moving with fear again. Regardless of what I thought or felt, God said "go" so I had to trust that He would make it turn out according to His plan.

We signed a contract for a space to accommodate fifty to eighty people, however, within two weeks, we sold 115 tickets. We could have sold hundreds more, but there wasn't any more space in the hotel for us! Look at God. Guess what? We didn't pay a dime in marketing. We had no celebrity endorsement. We didn't offer anything for free or make any promises. It was all God. When I walked into that room and saw all those unrecognizable beautiful faces looking back at me, smiling, I was floored! They were all so excited before I even said a word. I was overwhelmed. I thought "God is this real?" Is this really happening? After I composed myself, I did what I'd been doing for so many years before. I gave them the brunch experience of their life. It was a smashing success. So much so, that the ladies wanted to buy their tickets for the following year by the end of the brunch. The city that I was afraid to go to was saying, "You have to come back next year!"

From years of struggling to fill rooms to two sold-out cities in one year says, "Do not despise small beginnings." It was also a reminder that consistency pays off. What if I had stopped after year one or two? Each time I stepped out on faith and saw God move, it encouraged me to take even more significant steps. I then moved from two sold-out cities to a four-city tour-Raleigh, Atlanta, Charlotte, and Dallas in year nine. Would you believe all four cities sold out in less than thirty days? Four months before the actual event date we had over two hundred women excited to attend an event that was born over brunch with my girlfriends' years before.

Was all of it scary? Absolutely! However, if I stayed afraid and didn't "go" towards the thing that I was called to do, I would have been stagnant and missed a huge opportunity God already lined up for me. Like my friend and business partner Melissa says, "I'm not afraid of failure, I'm afraid of regret." Let me tell you, signing a contract for a considerable sum of money that you are on the hook for is no joke. You agree to be fully liable for this debt even if things don't happen as you planned. This takes real faith!

Even with that financial responsibility looming, one of my favorite sayings is "God will provide." I truly believe that. So what do I do? I get to work. I solicit all the help I need while praying for wisdom and direction. Then I thank God for the clarity, witty ideas, and His favor.

Do it again

Elevation Worship is one of my favorite worship groups. "Do it Again" is one of their most popular and my favorite worship song. The words seem to have been written just for me and my journey. A few lines of lyrics say:

> *"Walking around these walls*
> *I thought by now they'd fall*
> *But You have never failed me yet*
> *Waiting for change to come*
> *Knowing the battle's won*
> *For You have never failed me yet*
> *Your promise still stands*
> *Great is Your faithfulness, faithfulness*
> *I'm still in Your hands*

This is my confidence; You've never failed me yet
I know the night won't last
Your Word will come to pass
My heart will sing Your praise again
Jesus, You're still enough
Keep me within Your love
My heart will sing Your praise again
Your promise still stands
Great is Your faithfulness, faithfulness
I'm still in Your hands
This is my confidence, You never failed
Your promise still stands
Great is Your faithfulness, faithfulness
I'm still in Your hands
This is my confidence; You never failed me yet
I've seen You move, come move the mountains
And I believe, I'll see You do it again
You made a way, where there was no way
And I believe, I'll see You do it again…"
Endnote

For our 10th anniversary, we decided to do (drum roll) a ten-city tour! God has enlarged our territory. This means going into cities we've never been in and have no connections, hookups or audience. So I'm saying to God "You did it before, and I believe you will do it again." The reasons why I felt God put it in my heart to start and continue this journey has not changed. There are still women all around the world that need to be reached with this message of encouragement, connection, and sisterhood.

At the end of each brunch event, we were always asked, "When is the next event"? So we asked God "What's Next?" God directed us to what we call "Beyond the Brunch" experiences. Experiences that help us to fulfill more of our mission of creating lasting and meaningful connections such as Girlfriends Weekend, Girlfriends' Expo, and a Girlfriends Retreat.

Our event experiences are requested all over the country. As you can see, what started with fifty to fifty-five women is now a national brand. Yes, a national brand hosted by a woman with no following, name recognition, or endorsements. Someone with a heart to connect women simply trusting and following a big God. It is not where you start but where you finish. What has God called you to start, but you feel like you are not enough? Just remember that God can take the smallest things and turn them into large things beyond your wildest dreams.

God can take your crazy ideas and bring you covenant connections to help you turn that idea into a business. Selling tickets alone were not meeting all of our expenses. So God sent me help when I needed it most. With Melissa's help, we created a strategy to grow the business and bottom line. Then Melissa and I collaborated and wrote a book about what else - *The Gift of Girlfriends*. Next, we introduced a product line of tee shirts and mugs. We solicited sponsors to help with event costs. Who knows what God will download for us to do next? The thing is that we pray for witty ideas and we're open for where God leads us. So we are using what's in our hands and not just sitting on them. We believe, "Do the work and God will do the rest."

Is this what I'm supposed to be doing?

I'm often asked how did I know this is what I was supposed to be doing? Maybe you are asking yourself the same question. Here a few questions to help give you direction:

- Does it feel natural and not like work?

- If you never did it again would you be OK with that?

- Why do you want to do it?

- Is there room for God in it?

If you answer these questions honestly, then you will have your answers. For me, this is as natural as breathing. I couldn't imagine not doing this and it does not feel like a job. I used to think "this thing" I was doing that came so naturally to me was just a "cute" thing to do. The more I hosted the events, the more I could see it was a ministry, my God-ordained, God-Sized dream.

So again, I say to you, don't despise your small beginnings, your slow starts, or your crazy ideas. Don't worry about if someone else is doing it. There is room for you. People are waiting for you. You have something to bring to the masses that only you can deliver. Every city we go to, some women make their way to me and tell me how glad they are that I'm doing this. "This is so needed!" Then they say, "I will be here every year you come!" I think to myself, "what if I wasn't willing to do the work, or said no to things because I had to do "X" for the brunch"? Or "no one is doing this?" (which was the case when I started ten years ago) What if, what if, what if…would have kept me from my purpose.

I'm so glad I didn't quit and let the "what if's" keep me from moving forward. Now "this thing" is a multi-city and international thing. "This thing" attracts women that I would never have had a chance to meet otherwise. This thing is blessing women in ways beyond my understanding.

Never mind what things might look like on social media. Don't compare your chapter one with some else's chapter anything. Your God-Sized dream is just that - Yours! He who has begun a good work in you will complete it (Phil. 1:6). Keep dreaming, keep believing and keep working! As I embark on this ten-year, ten-city tour, I thought, "who told you that you could do this? It hasn't been done before. You don't have any endorsements. You don't have a celebrity backing. You don't have a huge Instagram following. You know all the things 'they' say you need to be successful." However, let me tell you this, God said that I could do this and His words to me are all that matter!

Lessons Learned

- When your name is on the line, check and double check everything. You are fully responsible for all that goes right or wrong.

- The faces in your tribe may change, but you always need a tribe!

- God will send you who and what you need when you are doing the work!

- Know your strengths and be honest about your weaknesses.

- Once you take the first step it becomes easier to take the next one!

- Ask God for what you want and as long as what you ask for is in alignment with His will, He will provide a way.

- Don't discount what comes naturally to you. It could be your ministry and the path to start your destiny.

God's Promises

In their hearts, humans plan their course, but the Lord establishes their steps. **Proverbs 16:9 (NLT)**

Do you see someone skilled in their work? They will serve before kings; they will not serve before officials of low rank. **(NIV)**

Be strong and courageous. Do not be afraid or terrified because of them, for the LORD your God goes with you; he will never leave you nor forsake you." **Deuteronomy 31:6 (NIV)**

Now Jabez called on the God of Israel, saying, "Oh that You would bless me indeed and enlarge my border, and that Your hand might be with me, and that You would keep me from harm that it may not pain me!" And God granted him what he requested." **1 Chronicles 4:10 (NIV)**

He has delivered us from such a deadly peril, and he will deliver us again. On him we have set our hope that he will continue to deliver us. **2 Corinthians 1:10 (NIV)**

Probing questions for you to consider when you feel like you are starting small:

What areas of your journey do you feel are small but you need to be more thankful for?

What areas of your journey do you feel are causing you delay in your progress?

What areas of your journey do you need to be committed to in spite of its size?

What is God calling you to do next that you have been afraid to do?

Prayer

Dear God,

I thank you that *everything* is significant in your eyes. Forgive me where I have discounted the very beginning stages of my journey and projects along the way. Even when I could not see how things were working in my favor with my natural eyes, you were always working behind the scenes on my behalf. You care about our first day with small beginnings just as much as you care about explosive results. Help me to remain steadfast (be faithful) to your promises/to your Word at each stage of the process. Help me know that you are always working everything together for my good no matter what (at every stage). I thank you for seasons of preparation as you groom me to be able to handle where I am going. I thank you for the faith to take the next step when it's time. I will walk in boldness in spite of fear. I will trust you more than I do my circumstances. I will look up to you more than I look out at what I can see. I believe that every beginning, every stage, every success is significant in your eyes. Thank you for being the One who makes all my dreams come true.

In Jesus Name,

Amen

If you are in the beginning of your journey, write you own prayer and/or affirmations below:

Chapter 4

Preparing Your Faith &
Finances

Nyisha Holliday

I will never forget the day that I finally said "yes" to my God-Sized dream. I am sure you can remember yours too and all that came with it. For me, it had been a whole year since I knew God was calling me to it, but this was the day I finally said "yes". My name is Nyisha Holliday and my background is full of variety. I wear a lot of hats from HR leader to a baker, preacher, landlord, coach, wife, and mom of three beautiful children.

I worked for fifteen years at the Federal Reserve Bank of New York in various leadership roles in Bank Supervision, Talent Management, and Diversity and Inclusion. All the while God was developing my faith and finances to prepare me to take the biggest leap of my professional life and pursue my God-Sized dream.

D Day – The deciding moment

It was Thursday, July 7th, 2016. I woke up that morning bright-eyed and bushy-tailed; well hydrated and rested. I had felt good the last few days but waited to make sure I didn't return to work too soon only to relapse and be out again. All of the boxes were checked to ensure that I was strong enough to go back to work. So I got up, got dressed, and sat down at my desk in my home office and logged in. Just as I was about to tell my boss I was back, out of nowhere, this all-too-familiar gut-wrenching pain shot through my hip and down my leg. I was horrified. I'm in crisis… AGAIN! Then, within my spirit, I heard, "Get the ID." This was *not* the word that I expected God to speak to me as I lay in the fetal position underneath my desk, cringing, and crying in pain.

Sobbing, discouraged, and confused; I had the audacity to be arguing with the God I desperately needed to hear from. "Lord… What's going on? I'm really trying to do right by work. I've done everything in my power to manage these sickle cell triggers. How can I ever be successful at work, if I am constantly out sick? How in the world am I supposed to be all that YOU called me to be and manage all that YOU'VE put in my hands if I am always in crisis? I have too much to do, and I'm already behind. Why aren't you helping me?!?!"

Yet, the anguish of my questions and the flow of my tears had little to do with the pain in my body or the extra time I'd need to take off to get myself together. All of my fears and insecurities were coming to bear. I sensed God was leading me to take the biggest leap of my career, but I wasn't certain it was him. I was terrified and continued with my questions.

Lord, is this you? I've rebuked the devil and pleaded the blood. I've done everything I know to do, but things are just getting worse. Are you leading me to leave my job? Because you know… I'm not **that** talented and I'm not **that** smart. I'm not **that** diligent and I'm not **that** resilient. I don't have enough money saved and I don't have enough connections. Lord… is this you?!?!"

To all of my hysteria, self-doubt, hostile interrogation, and river of tears…the Lord simply and softly replied, "Get the ID." OK, so before I go further, let me explain "the ID."

Twenty-three years earlier, I got pregnant with my oldest son, Kamari. I had become all of the things I said I would never be. I was somebody's baby mama, a single parent, a college dropout, and worst of all – a welfare recipient. I still remember the day I picked up my welfare card; I was eight months pregnant and disgusted. The Lord spoke to me that day and said, "Keep this ID, because where I am taking you and what I am going to do in your life, you won't remember that you were here. Others, who hear your testimony, won't believe that you were here either."

So, I buried the ID in an old file cabinet and went on with my life. Kamari was born. My career took off. I married my high-school sweetheart and "baby daddy." Together, we had two more beautiful children and purchased investment properties. I gave my life fully to Christ, and was called to preach the gospel. I had even launched a baking business. Things had turned out well.

So, when God said to "get the ID", I thought I knew where the conversation was going. I didn't just follow His instructions. No, I figured I would just have a conversation with Him about what He meant by what He said; cue the emoji of the girl with her hand over her face.

"OK, OK, I get it, Lord… I'm confused and scared about the decision to leave my job. Back then, I was confused and scared about the decision to have Kamari and you lead me, and it turned out great. OK, God, I get it."

To which the Lord replied, "Nyi… Get the ID". So I picked myself up off the floor, wiped my face, and made my way to the basement to get my old welfare ID.

When I took it out of the file cabinet, I couldn't believe what I saw. The date on the card was 7/07/93! I stood there in disbelief. At first, I thought, "this can't be right. Today must be July 8ᵗʰ, right?" I went upstairs and checked the date on my phone, I started bawling. It was July 7ᵗʰ, 2016… EXACTLY Twenty-Three years to the date and within the same hour that I had originally picked up my welfare ID!

Then, the Lord took over the conversation. "Nyi, I got you. I-got-you. I brought you through a dark season and blessed you when you were *wrong*, so don't be afraid to step out on what I'm telling you to do *now*. I know you don't understand it, and I know you want the details, but this time I'm giving you just enough faith for the step you are on. As you take a step, then the next step will be revealed. Then you take another step, and the next step will be revealed. But you don't get to have your own plan and strategy for *this*… No, for *this* you get to trust me."

That was the day I made the decision to leave my job of fifteen years and pursue my God- Sized dream. It would be another two months before I handed in my resignation. I spent that time recovering physically, getting clear on my next steps, and trying to answer the nagging questions that still flooded my heart. Even though I had made the decision, the fears and questions were still present. I still didn't feel prepared to take this leap.

What I didn't realize is that God had been preparing me for this moment for the last two decades. He had been using the most challenging, confusing, and painful events in my life to guide me, build my faith, and instill disciplines that prepared me for this moment. I couldn't see it before because I was blinded by fear and indecision. But for the next two months, I was able to see things clearer. I took inventory of the resources that were in my hand or at least within my reach. I put everything on the table to see how I could use or move what I had to support what I was about to do.

The money thing

"Don't seek financial advice from individuals who you wouldn't trade places with financially."

One of my biggest fears about taking the leap was how would I survive financially? This money thing seemed to be *the* thing to kill my God-Sized dream if I didn't get it right. I didn't have a lot of cash in my savings account, I wasn't going to receive severance pay, and since I was resigning, I was not eligible for unemployment. I had no idea how I'd continue to pay my bills *and* invest in a new business, so one of the first things I did was call my financial advisor, Mike Salley.

As an aside – it's important to have individuals who are experts in their field on your "personal board of trustees." These are people you consult with when making major financial decisions. These are professionals who have had success working in the world you have questions about. They are not necessarily friends and family members.

Whoever has your ear, has your head. They are guiding your decisions. Sometimes family and friends don't have the expertise that you need to go to the next level of your life. You may be poor because you are getting poor advice. Don't seek financial advice from individuals who you wouldn't trade places with financially. More importantly, don't seek financial advice from individuals who haven't demonstrated success in their own life.

Find people that you admire who have proven success in the area that you are looking to get advice. Ask people that you believe to be financially sound to introduce you to their experts. Many of the people that I consider to be on my team, I learned of them through referrals from people I respected. The point is, you need a team. You don't have to do this by yourself.

For me, Mike Salley fits the bill. He is a seasoned stock broker and a successful business owner who loves God and has taken me under his wing as a mentee. If anyone could give me some sage advice as I took this leap, it would be him.

I thought Mike was going to tell me to wait and save up a year's worth of living expenses, but to my surprise, he encouraged me to "do it now." When I pressed him about not having enough money saved, he showed me that while I didn't have a large cash savings, I *did* have quite a bit in my retirement fund and even more in equity in my rental properties. So we worked together to create a strategy that would help me access those funds.

I leveraged the equity in the rental properties to purchase a new rental in a lower income neighborhood. The new property would create a positive cash flow, enough to ensure my share of the bills were paid. In the meantime, I would become my own lender and borrow transition money from my retirement account. Even though I would have to pay the money back with interest, the good thing is that I am actually paying myself back.

You may be thinking, Nyi, that's good for you, but I don't have rental property or a significant retirement fund. How can I live my God-Sized dream and not go under financially? Don't worry, I didn't get there at the moment that God called me to my God- Sized dream, it took almost two decades. But I'm going to share financial principles with you that I've learned that you can use to put you in a position to live your God-Sized dream sooner than later.

Multiply it

I grew up financially illiterate. I didn't know anything about multiplying or managing money. The term "investments" and the concept of making money work for you were completely foreign to me. Even though I held jobs from the age of fifteen, I didn't have a checking account until I was well into my twenties. No one in my family used checking accounts and the only investments I had heard of was a susu.

So when Kamari's babysitter gave me and Phillip the first-time home buyers application, I wasn't too excited about it. We were just beginning to plan our wedding and if we were approved for the house, then we'd have to scale back the wedding. To make matters worse, the house was abandoned with trash up to the stoop level. The city was going to renovate it, but I definitely wanted a nice wedding over an abandoned house. I also didn't think that we would be approved. We had less than $2k between us and less than average credit scores.

But Phillip saw things differently. He knew that buying real estate, especially rental property was important. He convinced me to at least complete the application. So I did, and to my surprise, we were approved. We had to scale back the wedding and borrow money for the down payment; but 2 ½ years later we were standing in our newly renovated two-family brownstone in the hood of Bed-Stuy Brooklyn.

This would be one of the best financial decisions we would make – a gift that keeps on giving - but it sure didn't feel like it at the time. We had spent everything we had, and everything we could borrow to get into this house. We moved in with our clothes in garbage bags, my computer desk, and borrowed sheets that we put up to the window. Phillip and I slept on the living room floor on a blanket that I borrowed from my mother's house and Kamari had to stay with my mom until we could get furniture.

We were broke and scared. Without realizing it, we were on the road to financial freedom, but it felt like struggle. It felt like poverty. But buying that house taught me critical financial principles that I don't think I would have learned any other way.

I learned that wealth often begins in obscure places and with obscure ideas. To get a large return on your investment, you buy low – taking a risk on something that has potential, but doesn't look like much in the moment. You invest in what you see ahead and not what it appears to be now. Prophets make profit. You have to be willing to put your money and your time into things that will produce value later.

I also learned that the road to financial freedom isn't just about how hard you work to bring in income, but how you spend that income. The decision to spend on assets or liabilities makes a huge difference. Buying that property forced us to spend the bulk of our income on an asset. That meant that for a while we didn't have the resources to spend on niceties or conveniences. But years later, the value of that asset would multiply and be worth ten times what we paid for it.

The increase in property value wasn't the only benefit. It also allowed us to engage in "house hacking." That's when your investment property is also your primary residence, and the rental income from tenants covers most, if not all, of your housing expenses. For most of us, housing is our biggest expense, so house hacking is a game changer.

Even if you aren't ready to purchase rental property, there's good news. In today's market, there are several ways to take advantage of house hacking. You could offer short term rentals using sites like Airbnb, or you could rent your space to traveling executives or medical professionals. Or, you could just get a roommate. However you do it, house hacking can be a financial game changer.

Manage it

"The most important priority for me, was and still is my tithe."

Making that one good investment didn't mean that I was a good financial steward. I was not. I was casual about managing money. I lived haphazardly from paycheck to paycheck dealing with whatever bill was urgent at the time. I had no financial priorities (aside from the mortgage and my tithe) and I had no idea how much was coming in or going out. But that changed when I got into serious financial trouble. I learned to manage my money during one of the worst times of my financial life.

I had planned to take a year off of work after the birth of my second son, Josiah. I didn't have much of a financial plan, I just figured we'd be OK (don't judge me). Nothing was turned off and when I fell short, I used overdraft protection, credit cards, and tax returns to get us through. I figured I'd clean up any financial issues once I went back to work. I didn't expect to get pregnant…again! But that's what happened.

When Josiah was seven months old, I found out that I was pregnant with our daughter Imani. To further complicate things, our tenant was not paying rent, and we had to hire a lawyer to get her out. During the same time, my mom had gotten sick and was coming to stay with us. So, there I was: out of work, pregnant, and with almost $20K worth of debt. My family size was doubling, expenses were increasing, and our income was down by 70%.

Things were getting really bad. The creditors were calling and were very nasty. Every time I saw an 800- number come up on the caller ID, my heart sank, my stomach turned, and I would just stare at the answering machine in terror as they left yet another threatening message. Kamari had to go to the poorly rated public school because we couldn't afford his tuition. I didn't know how I would pay the bills or more importantly, feed my children. I was severely depressed and had started entertaining suicidal thoughts. It felt like it was all my fault and I was helpless to fix it.

But I talked to one of my sisters in Christ, my friend and mentor, Sis Tina. She sat me down and taught me to take control of my finances. She helped me see that even though I wasn't working, I could make a positive impact on my household finances.

I first learned to prioritize. I categorized our expenses as "needs" or "wants" and then I put the needs in order of importance. The most important priority for me was and still is my tithe. The first 10% of our income went to God. I didn't know a lot about managing money but I knew that I needed God to help me. I knew that tithing was an indication of my faith and my respect for God. I knew that it was a requirement if I was going to receive God's abundance and break this generational financial curse over my life.

Tithing tends to get a bad rap, but there were critical benefits for me as a believer. It broke a poverty mindset that caused me to see myself as helpless and needy. It put me in a position of power to be able to give to a cause greater than me. It acts as an insurance policy for my money. God protects me from the enemy who attempts to destroy me financially (See Malachi 3:11). Tithing also helps to ensure that God is *the* priority in my life and that I don't fall prey to the love money or the deceitfulness of riches. This is a faith walk and I have to make sure that my actions are aligned with my belief.

But tithing alone was not enough. I had mismanaged the other 90% and as a result, despite my tithe, I was broke. God could not trust me with more because I hadn't managed what I had. If He had given me more, I would have wasted more. I would have used it for my own convenience, indulgence, or appearance (the CIA as Dave Ramsey calls it). I would have spent it and continued to dig a financial hole for myself and my family.

So to better manage the 90%, I first learned to reduce costs. If it wasn't a need, it had to go. That meant fast food was a thing of the past. The cell phone, cable, and phone features were all turned off. Back then, you had to pay extra for Call Waiting and Caller ID. I stopped all unnecessary banking fees. I used only the free ATMs, cancelled the overdraft protection, and began tracking our expenses to ensure that we didn't go into the negative. Tina also told me about the government FAN program. A place where I could get basic groceries for free. I was embarrassed, but reducing my grocery bill and feeding my children was more important than my pride.

Then I had to face my creditors. I had to actually open the letters they sent me and answer their phone calls, even though they were nasty. I had to be honest about my situation and negotiate payment terms until I was able to return to work. Some accepted my very small payments, but others charged off my balance. My credit was taking a beating, but at least I had my integrity. At least I wasn't hiding anymore. I was living and speaking my financial truth and dealing with the consequences.

Then Imani was born, and within 3 months I had gotten hired at the Federal Reserve Bank of New York. Things would be very different. I was determined to *never* be in that financial situation again. I was going to get this money thing right no matter what. And now that I had steady income, I could make an even greater difference in our home.

For the first year, I focused on getting out of debt. I believed that I was supposed to be the lender and not the borrower (Deut. 28:12). So, I decided to pay my lenders like *I* was the lender. Each time I got paid, I took out my tithing and my carfare, and used the rest to pay my credit cards. I was used to going without, so I decided to wait to start spending on niceties. By making multiple payments each month, my credit score started to improve significantly. At the end of the first year, I had paid off $20k in debt.

When I started at the Fed, I immediately took advantage of their savings and retirement plan. I had read that you should put at least 10% of your earnings toward retirement, so that's what I did. It was an automatic deduction from my paycheck, so I didn't miss it. After all, I had gone without a paycheck for a couple of years, I was just happy to have an income.

Investing in my retirement fund had other benefits. The higher my investment, the lower my taxes. So, for several years I had upwards of 15% coming out of my check. The Fed also matched my contributions up to 6%. To not invest in my retirement was to leave free money on the table. Even if the market went down a bit, I had a 6% cushion before I lost any of my own money. If you're unable to pay 10% towards your retirement, start small, then increase it by 1% each year. You'll barely notice a difference.

I also started planning and forecasting my expenses. It seemed like we were going along fine and then every few months we would get hit with what I thought were "unexpected expenses" and "emergencies" that could wipe out our savings or force us to use credit cards. But as I started taking time to write out a budget, I started thinking about what was coming up the following month. I started paying attention to those "unexpected expenses" and "emergencies."

Turns out, they weren't really unexpected, they just weren't monthly. Emergencies don't feel like emergencies when you see them coming and prepare for them. Cars need maintenance, so brake pads and oil changes are inevitable. Every August, the kids needed school clothes and supplies. Doctors' visits are yearly and colds happen regularly. Birthdays and holidays happen at the same time every year. Planning for these events required me to put a few extra line items in my budget. It cost me very little each month. But it helped to make sure I wasn't making financial decisions in a panic or based upon my emotions.

To further ensure that I was making clear-headed financial decisions, I automated some of my expenses. I even got a discount from my car insurance carrier for allowing automatic deductions. I took advantage of a flexible spending account. I estimated what my yearly medical expenses would be (i.e. copays, OTC medicines, dental visits, eyeglasses, etc.). My employer made small pretax deductions from each paycheck. Then, when an expense came up, I could put in a claim and use the pretax money to pay it.

Later, I learned to use direct deposit to split my paycheck between three accounts: an operating account, a savings account, and a discretionary account. I had gotten a lot better at managing money, but I didn't want to put myself in the position to make financial decisions based upon my emotions. I needed to add another layer of protection from *me*. I also wanted to reduce the time that I needed to spend managing and tracking my expenses.

I used the operating account for stable bills like household expenses and car payments. I didn't carry that debit card or checkbook with me. I used an online account for my savings. They pay a higher interest rate compared to my commercial bank. There is no debit card and to access the funds takes three business days. This protects me from making large impulse purchases. Since I have to wait for the money, I have time to think it through. I use the discretionary account for fluctuating expenses, conveniences and the occasional indulgence. This is the debit card and checkbook that I carry. It makes sure that these discretionary expenses never interfere with my household expenses or my savings.

My finances were finally in a stable place and then the Lord began to nudge me about leaving the Fed to launch my own business. I did everything I could to ignore him. I didn't want to do anything that would jeopardize my financial stability. I had been there, done that, and I wasn't going back. But I was about to begin a faith walk. It wasn't going to be comfortable, but it wasn't going to sink me either. Where I had been, had prepared me for where I was going.

Faith cometh… the process of getting to "Yes Lord"

It took more than a year for me to build the faith I needed to say yes to my God-Sized dream. At first things were going well at work, but it started to change when I was exposed to the possibility of life outside of the Fed. I had gotten my John Maxwell Certification and had become a part of a community of thousands of individuals who were making a living as speakers and coaches. I also began developing relationships with the trainers and consultants that the Fed hired. These new relationships were fueling an old desire to work more fully in the area of my gifting. I wanted to spend more time coaching, training, and speaking but even though I was in HR, the opportunities to do so were becoming less frequent.

I was beginning to grow weary and frustrated with the job that I once loved. I looked forward to Friday afternoons and dreaded Sunday nights. I found myself daydreaming in staff meetings. When others were excited to plan the next project, I was bored and uninterested. I kept asking myself, "Why am I here?" knowing that the answer was simply, "for the paycheck." I was losing the grace to do what I used to enjoy and do with ease.

But I was not a novice. I had twenty-three years of professional experience under my belt. I had hit rough patches before. So I did what I knew to do. I kept regular meetings with my boss to make sure I was addressing his priorities. I got advice from mentors and began networking to find new and interesting projects to work on. None of it worked. I was getting weary with my job and the desire to do more outside of the Fed was growing.

Yet, I continued to try to make it work. I tried to think positively and be grateful for the job that I had. I encouraged myself to do a good job, no, a great job on my projects. And when that didn't work, I started putting in applications at other companies. Strangely enough, that didn't work either. This was getting frustrating. I had always been able to find a job, so why was it a problem all of a sudden?

As I was exposed to opportunities outside of the Fed, I was also hearing a recurring word in church that it was "time to leave your job." Initially, I rejected it. I knew it was a word from God, but I didn't think it was for me. For a while, I was happy at work. I had a great position, I was making six figures, had great benefits, and the luxury of working from home. Great Word, but not for me.

But the more I heard it, the more that Word resonated with me. I was beginning to believe that the Lord was nudging me to take a leap of faith, but I didn't know how I would do it. My fear and my faith were both growing. It was a confusing time.

One moment I was in church and sure that I was leaving my job. Then at home in the middle of the night I'd wake up in a cold sweat and heart pounding trying to convince myself to stay put.

I'd tell myself things like "you are absolutely insane"; "who just up and leaves their job making six figures? "Why don't you just cut it out and go to work like everyone else?" Then the inner voice got vicious and personal, "You are just being a coward and running away when you should stay and endure. You are going to destroy everything you have worked for over the last twenty years. You and your family are going to be poor and homeless. This isn't God, this is just your flesh. You are prideful to think that you can leave the job that God gave you!"

As an aside, be careful of the voice in your head that constantly accuses you. It can hide behind the desire for excellence and the desire to please God. God doesn't accuse you. He will correct you and even chastise you, but He does not mock or condemn you. That voice is the voice of the enemy of your soul. He is using God's invitation for you to do and be more as an occasion to torment you.

I didn't realize it, but somewhere along the way I had lost my faith, at least the kind of game changing faith that I needed for the next phase of my life. I didn't backslide or anything. It was quite the opposite. I was in church every Sunday and Tuesday. While I am definitely not perfect, I lived all that I knew how to please God. I even taught Bible school classes and counselled members of my church on their own spiritual development. I wasn't a hypocrite, but I wasn't ready for my next level either.

None of my efforts to fix and manage the situations in my life required faith. I knew how to navigate corporate America to move ahead. I knew how to get another job. I could do those things with very little risk. I was still getting paid and I still had benefits. They were familiar strategies that kept me comfortable. I was doing what I had always done, but God was moving in a different direction. He was teaching me the faith to step out.

Then, I started having frequent sickle cell crises. While I was born with the disease, it had only become an issue over the last few years. For most of my life, it was just something that I had to mention to doctors when they asked about my medical history. But now, the crises were increasing with the frequency and with the intensity of childbirth. Every time I seemed to be making progress at work, I'd get another sickle crisis. I'd be out for a week, and then two weeks, and then a month. It was like some cruel joke.

All of this back and forth, faith and fear, progress and crisis continued until that fateful Thursday when I finally said yes and decided to take the leap of faith.

Answering the call – my rsvp

This faith walk is a process. It's not a one and done scenario. In my case, it was a series of steps, and conversations, and situations between me and the Lord. So even though I had made the decision to leave my job, my journey was just beginning. If I was going to accept His invitation, I needed to know if I could really do it. I had to be sure this was really Him and not my anxiety and frustration. So for the next two months, through prayer and study, He began to teach me and answer my most pressing questions. He laid out the next steps to prepare me for the journey.

The faith to step out

Lord is this you? One of the areas the enemy tormented me in was not knowing for sure if this leap was God or my flesh. I needed to know that it was not the result of my own ambition or vain desires. God used the story of Peter walking on water to settle my soul and assure me that this move was not outside of His will (See Matthew 14:22-32 NIV).

As the story goes, the disciples had followed Jesus' command, and ended up in a ship, in the middle of the sea, and in a storm. Jesus showed up walking on the sea. Peter asked, "Lord if it's you, allow me to come to you on the sea" (*vs. 28 paraphrased*). Jesus told him to come. Peter walked on water and then started to sink. Jesus reached out his hand and saved him. They both end up back in the ship and the sea had calmed.

I learned a couple of valuable lessons from that story. When Peter saw Jesus walking on water it created a desire in him to do more. He could have asked Jesus to get into the ship, but instead he asked if he could come to Jesus on the water. When we are exposed to greatness, it creates a desire in us that we would not have had otherwise. Psalms 37:4 *paraphrased* says that if we delight ourselves in the Lord, He will give us the desires of our hearts. That's not just giving us what we already want, it's an indication that He would put Godly desires in us. Furthermore, because I needed a lot of assurance, Philippians 2:13 says, "For God is working in you, giving you the desire and the power to do what pleases Him" (NLT). So the desire that I had to help people and to start a business was a good thing, and it was also a God thing.

Peter walking on water, wasn't about him walking on water at all. It was about him experiencing our Lord in a whole new way. It takes another level of faith to step out and experience the Lord on the water *in a storm*, than it does to wait in the boat until He comes. You have a deeper level of intimacy and you learn some things by experience that you'd never learn by watching. Therefore, the desire to do more must be coupled with the desire for God. Peter ultimately was trying to get more of Jesus.

Like Peter, I wanted a deeper walk with the Lord, and I wanted to leave my job. I had an opportunity and a choice. There were eleven other disciples on the ship who did nothing with what Peter saw as an opportunity. They were not cursed, and they were not bad people, but they would never have the kind of relationship with the Lord that Peter had and they would not become the chief bishop of the first church.

Peter had a lot of flaws but ended up being the presiding prelate of the first church. He was a loud mouth who spoke out of turn. He cursed, he cut a man that Jesus had to heal, and he denied our Lord three times. But even with all of his flaws, he still ended up in the highest level of leadership in the first church. I believe something unique happened when Peter walked on water. It showed that he had the kind of faith that would trust God enough to step out, take action, and do impossible things in the midst of a storm. This kind of relationship with the Lord qualified him for leadership.

The other thing I learned from this story is that even if I stepped out and messed up, the Lord would save me. When Peter started to sink, he cried out to Jesus, and our Lord saved him. What a blessed assurance that is. It settled my spirit to understand that God is my loving father and He won't let me drown. If I go too far, or if I'm in some way off, He will chastise me and correct me, but He will save me. It's His nature to save me.

To be clear, that's not a license to deliberately mess up, or to be cavalier with opportunities, or to be overly ambitious. However, I hope it reassures you, like it does me, that once again, God's got me. Whether right or wrong, weak or strong, my Father is with me. The scripture reminded me that God is with me, wherever I go (See Joshua 1:9 NIV).

God gives us opportunities and choices, but it's up to us to take them. If we go back to the Garden of Eden, we understand that there was only one tree that was forbidden. They could eat of all the rest, freely. It was their choice. We often focus on what we can't or shouldn't do. But I encourage you to start seeing all of the things that you *can* do. I encourage you to look at what's in your hand, and what's possible (even if it seems impossible). Make a choice, knowing that God's got you too.

It's not about you

Can I really do it? This question was at the root of my insecurity and the tool the enemy used to torment me. Even after I made the decision to leave my job, I had moments of anxiety where I questioned my ability to do the darn thing. So I didn't know if I *should* do it, because I didn't know if I *could* do it. I had conversations with my accountant and my financial advisor. They both thought I *could* and *should* launch my own business. I had conversations with girlfriends who had successfully left corporate America and they all thought I could do it too. Everyone seemed to be clear about my next career move… except me.

But I'm so glad that God didn't leave me to the devices of the enemy. During yet another one of my anxious fits He spoke four simple words that would carry me through my journey. He said simply, "It's not about you."

Normally, we say this phrase to someone who we think is self-seeking and conceited. They are in a situation where they can't, or won't, look at it from someone else's perspective. But when God spoke these words to me, I thought I was walking in humility. Instead, I was really being self-absorbed. There was a subtle, yet powerful shift that I needed to make. I needed to see it from God's perspective and through the perspective of those I was called to serve.

All of my insecurities and fears had been about *me*. What would happen to *me* if I stepped out and messed up? It was all about what I was missing, what was wrong with me, and what I was lacking. Those four words freed my soul. This was a faith walk, so it was about my ability to hear and obey, rather than my skills and expertise. It also wasn't about my hang-ups and insufficiencies. In fact, I didn't have a hang-up or an insufficiency that could disqualify me from being me, or from doing what He called me to do.

He knew all about me and what I was lacking *before* He called me. Truth be told, He didn't choose me *in spite* of my weaknesses, but He chose me *because* of them! He chose me in my weakened state to be sure that I would not take credit for His work. He took an assessment of me and decided that what was wrong with me was a perfect canvas for His glory. He reminded me of the Scripture in 1 Corinthians 1:27-29 that says:

But God hath chosen the foolish things of the world to confound the wise; and God hath chosen the weak things of the world to confound the things which are mighty; And base things of the world, and things which are despised, hath God chosen, yea, and things which are not, to bring to nought things that are: That no flesh should glory in his presence. (KJV)

Build an altar

"When you do better, you know better."

As I began the process of my development, the Lord said to me, "Before you build a business, before you build a ministry or a family, build an altar." I was instructed to find every scripture that the Lord had spoken over my life and recall His specific words to me. I was to print them out, frame them, and post them on my wall. I needed a space that would be a shield and a sanctuary for my soul. A place or space to go to when the enemy came against me. I needed a place that would immediately remind me of what God said. Because His Word is my defense and my strength.

Next, I was admonished to make simple changes in seemingly unrelated areas. I had to get excellent and efficient at some very menial tasks and some basic spiritual practices that were crucial to securing my success. First, I had to ensure that I was taken care of physically and spiritually. Then, I had to ensure that my family's needs were met. Finally, I had to create routines that would keep me creative and productive.

For me, I had to relearn to do simple things. Normally, I am in bed by 10:30 PM so that I wake up by 5:30 AM. Getting up early allows me the quiet time and space to take care of *me* before I take care of everyone else. I can pray, read, and study so that my head and my heart are in a good place to serve others. I put a large bottle of water on my nightstand so that it's the first thing I drink in the morning. Staying hydrated is crucial to avoiding sickle crises.

I had to be intentional about taking care of my husband and family. I created chore schedules and blocked off time to just hang out and watch our favorite shows. I scheduled my work times around Phillip's schedule. On the days that he was home, I might only spend two hours working on my business. I knew that I could make up the time when he was at work. I want to be successful in business and ministry, but I also want a happy home. I wasn't making this shift alone, so I had to make sure that my family was good and on board as I transitioned.

Finally, I had to put simple systems in place. I cleaned up my papers and created a better system to keep things in order. I scheduled time to do my budget and pay bills. I started using simple tools like the calendar on my phone, a small dry-erase board, and a journal. I put all events (business, personal, church, etc.) in the calendar and made sure that my family members had it on their calendars too. I used the whiteboard to keep a short-term to-do list visible. I check off what's completed as the day goes on.

Most importantly, I started spending time reflecting and planning. At the end of each day, I check to see what I've done and write down what needs to be done for the next day. The journal helps me reflect on how I felt about what happened that day. What went well, what didn't go according to plan, and what things I can do differently. It clears my head so that I don't go to bed with my mind racing. It helps me wake up refreshed.

I know these things don't seem like they are relevant to building faith, but they are. Don't ignore them. This kind of basic preparation did a couple of things for me. It created the structure I needed to handle what God was doing. It reinforced a spirit of humility and a servant's heart so that God could trust me with great things. Finally, it quieted some of the insecurities that I had about making this transition.

Until you do it, the enemy can torment you with the possibility that you can't do it. But as you prepare, do the work, and see the results – even in small ways, it builds your faith in God, and in the God in *you*. It's been said that when you know better, you do better. I like to say that when you do better, you know better. Doing the work helps you to know that *you* "can do all things through Christ who strengthens" *you* (Phil. 4:13).

Activating the dream

Finally, the day had come for me to put in my resignation. I had a meeting scheduled with my boss that afternoon and decided to tell him then. I was nervous all day. I didn't know how I'd feel once it was done. This had been such a long and intense process I thought I might have a meltdown when it was finally done. But I didn't.

Once I told my boss that I was leaving, once it was final, I felt a strange sense of peace. I felt a surge of confidence and relief. While I was nervous about what the future held, I was excited and humbled to be able to make this transition.

Life After Corporate America

Since I've left the Fed, God has done some pretty amazing things. Some things He did through my efforts and as I stepped out. Then there were other opportunities that were just placed in my lap.

So far, I've launched *Play to Win Coaching and Development Services*. I've been a featured conference speaker and developed and launched courses including *Play to Win, Mastering Your Mindset, and Developing Your Game-plan*. I've helped authors, emerging coaches, ministry leaders, and go-to girlfriends get past their self-limiting beliefs, monetize their talents, and impact the marketplace. I've also had the privilege of coaching several clients through their own transition from a 9-to-5 into full time entrepreneurship and ministry.

I've launched an online community called *Saved and Wealthy*. I teach believers principles to achieve financial freedom. The purpose is to create a community of believers who live abundantly, give freely, and use their resources to live out their purpose.

In addition, I've also had the opportunity to host the first season of a TV Show called "365 Dream." I held on-air coaching sessions with guests to help them design a unique strategy to prepare for and execute their dream.

To my surprise, Phillip retired earlier than expected. Together we are expanding our real estate portfolio. We've purchased a fourth property and are in the process of doing our first full gut renovation. We will use it as rental property. We've even had the privilege of performing relationship coaching together. We've coached married couples on developing *one voice and one vision* for their home. It's a program that helps couples get past barriers, strengthen their communication, and get on the same page.

This has been such a fantastic journey. Although it hasn't been what I thought it would be and there have been lots of challenges along the way. But I can honestly say that I wouldn't change *anything* and boy am I enjoying my journey!

What's next?

As far as I can see, I will continue grow *Play to Win*, conducting individual and group coaching sessions, training programs, and speaking engagements. I will continue to expand my online community and host a *Saved and Wealthy Conference*. I will author two books: *Play to Win* and *Saved and Wealthy*. I will also continue to expand my real estate portfolio. Additionally, I want to spend more time serving on the Marriage Ministry and in the Bible School of my local church. Only God knows where we will truly end up. But I am excited about the possibilities.

Lessons Learned

- God doesn't always give details. Sometimes He gives you just enough faith for the step you are on. It's not to frustrate you, but rather to teach you to trust Him.

- Trust the process because it's priceless. Don't worry too much about what you don't have. The process is designed to help you grow into the things that are missing.

- Relax, God's got you. Trust Him with *all* of you.

- Hack your housing expenses. Rent to a tenant, a roommate, a professional, or a traveler.

- Prophets make profit.

- Wealth often begins in obscure places with obscure ideas.

- You may be poor because you are getting poor advice.

- You don't have a hang-up or an insufficiency that can disqualify you from being you, or from doing what God called you to do.

- If you always do what you've always done, you'll always be who you always were.

- When you step out of the norm, you will not only change the game for yourself, but for your children, your family, and everyone connected to you. More people are watching your life than you know. So go for it. It's helping them too.

- This faith walk is a journey. There are some things that God does immediately. But faith comes… it is a process. Enoch walked with the Lord until he was not. You have to walk with the Lord long enough until what you used to be is no longer. You walk with the Lord until you step into your next dimension. Until what was, is not.

God's Promises

- And we know that all things work together for good to them that love God, to them who are the called according to his purpose. **Romans 8:28 (NIV)**

- But God chose the foolish things of the world to shame the wise; God chose the weak things of the world to shame the strong. God chose the lowly things of this world and the despised things—and the things that are not—to nullify the things that are, so that no one may boast before him. **1 Corinthians 1:27-29 (NIV)**

- For God is working in you, giving you the desire and the power to do what pleases him. **Philippians 2:13 (NLT)**

- For I can do everything through Christ, who gives me strength. **Philippians 4:13 (NIV)**

- Bring the whole tithe into the storehouse, that there may be food in my house. Test me in this, says the Lord Almighty, and see if I will not throw open the floodgates of heaven and pour out so much blessing that there will not be room enough to store it. I will prevent pests from devouring your crops, and the vines in your fields will not drop their fruit before it is ripe, says the Lord Almighty. **Malachi 3:10-11 (NIV)**

- And my God will meet all your needs according to the riches of his glory in Christ Jesus. **Philippians 4:19 (NIV)**

- For we live by faith, not by sight. **2 Corinthians 5:7 (NIV)**

- For in the gospel the righteousness of God is revealed—a righteousness that is by faith from first to last, just as it is written: The righteous will live by faith. **Romans 1:17 (NIV)**

- But remember the Lord your God, for it is he who gives you the ability to produce wealth, and so confirms his covenant, which he swore to your ancestors, as it is today. **Deuteronomy 8:18 (NIV)**

- Keep this Book of the Law always on your lips; meditate on it day and night, so that you may be careful to do everything written in it. Then you will be prosperous and successful. **Joshua 1:8 (NIV)**

- Trust in the Lord with all your heart and lean not on your own understanding; in all your ways submit to him, and he will make your paths straight. **Proverbs 3:5-6 (NIV)**

Probing questions for you to consider when preparing your faith and finances:

Consider the painful, frustrating, disappointing areas in your life. What lessons might you learn from them? What might God be teaching you?

Remember a situation from your past in which you exercised faith. How did it turn out? What did you take away from the experience?

What has been a recurring Word that you've heard from God, whether it is coming across the pulpit or in your heart?

What's in your hand? What talents do you have? Is God getting a return on His investment in you?

How can you prepare for your God-Sized dream?

What is your money saying about what you love? What will you do to ensure your financial foundation is secure?

Prayer

Lord, thank you for being our father and for calling us your own. Thank you for the privilege to talk to you about our heart's desires and fears. Thank you for ordering our steps in your Word. Thank you for being patient and kind while we are going through your process. In this moment, I bow my head and bring my thoughts under subjection to your Word. I bend my knee in submission to your will. I thank you because you are All Sufficient, even when we don't feel like we are enough. Without you we are nothing, but with you we are enough, and we can do anything.

Father I pray for my sister who is reading this now. I rebuke the torment of the enemy that would attempt to thwart your plan in her life. I come against every devil and every demonic force that is coming against her. Satan, we see your strategy, and we decree and declare that it will not work. The blood of Jesus is against you, and that blood covers her now. Father, your Word says perfect love casts out fear. I pray that your love would sweep through her heart. Settle her spirit, even if you don't answer her prayer right away. Give her the kind of peace that passes all understanding and guards her heart through you.

Father, open her eyes that she can see you in the midst of the chaos. Help her to see what's in her hand. Help her to understand the wealth of your inheritance in her. You do all things well. We humble ourselves and recognize that all things are under your control. Even if you didn't send it, you allowed it. And if you allowed it, somehow, someway you are going to work it for our good and for your glory! So we bless you in it, and we bless you because of it.

Help us to know your will for our lives, help us to see our situation the way you see it.

We thank you for sending your Word and increasing our faith. We thank you that regardless of what it looks like, the enemy did not triumph!

Father, give her the boldness and the humility it takes to step out and walk in the next level of faith. Give her the courage she needs to do what's in her heart. Continue to give us Godly desires and courageous faith, that you might be glorified in the Earth.

To you be all glory and honor, forever.

In Jesus' name I pray,

Amen

Insert your prayer and/or affirmations for your faith and finances here:

Chapter 5

Building Your God-Sized Dream While Working a 9-to-5

Kimberly Hall

What happens when you've achieved a highly successful career, but you still are not fulfilled?

You don't know, what you don't know…

During the summer of 1983, I was accepted into Cass Technical High School in Detroit, Michigan. Being accepted into Cass Tech was a big deal. It's a university preparatory school, located in downtown, Detroit. I ran into my parent's bedroom full of joy and excitement and announced that I wanted to be a fashion designer. I had no idea what I needed to major in and I asked if I should grab the encyclopedias to start researching. My parents thought I was joking and they laughed. After they realized I was serious, they sat me down for "the talk".

My mom and dad proceeded to tell me that I had to select a major that would get me a good job and one that would make me successful. In my parents' eyes, it was so obvious that I had to major in Business. My mom, the math teacher, gave me a ton of statistics on the likelihood of me ending up in New York as a fashion designer. They asked me to look around the house and told me that life, as I knew it would not be the same. I was encouraged to have fashion design as a hobby, as careers in the arts were for a select few.

I thought to myself, "maybe they were right. Maybe my desire to create and design was unrealistic." I spent the next four years taking business classes and I went on to major in accounting in college. After college, I took jobs in accounting and finance. Month end close, financial statements and analysis was the only life I knew, and there was nothing creative or inspirational about it.

My unicorn

Eat, work, family, sleep & REPEAT. That was my daily activity in my 20's and early 30's. I was a young mother with a demanding job as a Sr. Cost Accountant and had a husband who was a unicorn (at least in my eyes). I didn't know anyone, other than him, that loved what they did and didn't feel like their job was work. Clearly, he missed the memo that a job is not supposed to be something you are passionate about. Your passion is your hobby and you don't make money from your hobby, right? He would ask me lots of questions about what I was interested in, what made me happy outside of family, and what would I do, if I weren't afraid. I had no idea. So many thoughts were running through my mind: *What is my purpose? What am I passionate about? Should I go back to school? How do I reconcile this? Is it possible to have a job that you love?*

My life was shaken

In late May 2001, the Accounting Department went through a reduction in workforce. Six people lost their jobs and everyone was on pins and needles, wondering who was next. On June 8, 2001, the Human Resource Manager pulled me out of a meeting. Walking down the hall to the conference room, I was thinking to myself, "I am losing my job". As I walked into the conference room and saw two Navy officers in uniform, my heart felt like it was beating through my chest. I dropped to my knees and said softly, "Please, just tell me he's hurt". The CACO (Casualty Assistance Calls Officer) said, "Ma'am I can't tell you that". I was informed that my husband had been involved in a fatal plane crash, while doing what he loved, flying. My greatest fear was now my reality. I felt as if I had an out of body experience that day. I've never experienced such pain and loss in my life. I was so angry with GOD. How could he allow this to happen? I was supposed to grow old with my unicorn, yet I only had him for a few years. For many weeks, I was concerned about my 9-year-old son, as he rarely cried or showed any emotions.

Late one night, I got up to get some water and I could hear him whimpering. I went into his room and he was crying. I crawled into bed with him and he apologized for crying.   He said he was now the man of the house and he was going to take care of me and didn't want me to see him crying. At that moment I realized, I had to pull myself together and take care of my son. He needed me to be fully present. He needed me to be a parent. He needed me now more than ever. In reality, we both needed each other, yet my heart was screaming in pain.

The healing powers of paper

I didn't think I'd ever be happy again. All I knew was that I wanted to hold on to every memory that I could. So in the lonely months that followed, I found solace in the creative hours I spent alone. Working with paper and old photos, pens and journals, I reminisced over my life. I fell in love with the healing power of old photos glued to a page and words inked on the paper. Scrapbooking and journaling are what kept me sane. What started out as a journal full of anger, pain and woe is me, later turned into thankfulness for the time I had with my unicorn.

My journaling began to transform into a grateful and thankful journal, as I had a lot to be thankful for. My main focus during those years was to make sure my son was healthy, happy, excelling in school and experiencing a life full of new experiences. It was important for me that we lived in the moment and not put off places and people we wanted to see, as we truly knew what the phrase, "here to today, gone tomorrow" meant.

I scrapbooked every event in my son's life, including his soccer tournaments, travels to Australia, Europe, South Africa and even his obsession with animals. It meant and still means so much to capture these wonderful memories in books and cards. Although technology was changing and creating less human interactions, due to increasing social media, I was adapting slowly. Trust me, I was kicking and fighting the entire time.

During those years, I grew closer to my mother. Let's just say we weren't the best of friends in high school. She was very strict, set in her ways and I was truly a daddy's girl. Daddy could do no wrong. My parents divorced when I was twenty-four and I started to see another side of my mother that I hadn't seen before. She was vulnerable and shared more of herself. My mother knew the wilderness and darkness I experienced, although she didn't talk about it much. Her father killed her mother, when I was a baby. My mother never talked about her pain, but I could see it in her eyes, when I asked questions about my grandmother, who I had no recollection of.

The one thing that always bothered me was that my mother only had two or three pictures of her mother. My mother didn't have very many photos of her siblings and her growing up at a young age. I wanted to do everything I could to make up for not having these visible memories. I made her scrapbooks of my brother and me growing up. I made her books every year of her only grandson growing up. My mother loved all of these memories and she looked forward to them. Creating memories has always been what makes me happy.

Percolation in process

My son was growing up to be a wonderful young man and he was truly passionate about wanting to be a veterinarian. The way his eyes lit up talking about animals made my heart melt. I made sure I exposed him to any and everything I could when it came to animals, culture and travel. I was thrilled that he was pursuing what made him happy and finding his lane. It was the spark that I needed to leave *my* comfort zone. It was time that I figured out my own passion and what made *me* happy.

In the Spring of 2007, I went to the VP of Sales at my company and asked to be considered for a job in Marketing & Sales. There had to be creativity in this career, right? It was definitely outside of my comfort zone, but I was willing to take a risk. With my finance background and my strength in building relationships, I started attending customer meetings with the Sales Director. Later that year, I transitioned into a job as a National Account Manager. I did extremely well in that role, yet something was still missing. I had not discovered my purpose in life, and it was still the missing piece that I had not figured out.

Slowly and bravely finding my strength

In the fall of 2010, my son left for college. I now had a lot of time for exploration. It was time to leave my comfort zone again, but this time physically. I'd never played sports, but had always worked out at the gym, so I thought, *why not push my body to new levels*? I decided to sign up for my first triathlon. In a triathlon, you swim, bike and run. There was something about running that felt natural and therapeutic. I decided to run more often and it felt amazing. Running became my place of solace and reflection. What began as a few miles a week, turned into forty-plus full and half marathons. I was amazed at what my body could do. I began to feel like a badass on the pavement and at work!

I continued to scrapbook my life and running journey as I found my "badass-ness." It was nothing for me to stop during a race and capture a moment with my camera. It wasn't all about the race time for me, it was about the experience. I was becoming comfortable in my skin and I loved every minute of it. This once skinny, tall, self-conscious girl was now a runner. Then it hit me, *I'm a freaking athlete!* Something felt so good about feeling like an athlete. Life was good.

False start, but it's a start

Feeling confident, motivated, and ready to take on new challenges, I started to read more self-help books while taking "starting small business classes" at the local community college. There are two things that I love for sure: working with paper and running. How can I make scrapbooking or running into a career? Opening a fitness center, creating scrapbooks for others, or can I combine the two? How do I figure this out? Education is power, but I needed help.

I reached out to a Life Coach and we started working on understanding my strengths and weaknesses through assessments and 360's. The information was valuable, but I still wasn't sure what I needed to do with it. At this point, I felt confused. Do I find another job in Corporate America? Buy a business franchise or create one? I started to pray and ask God to reveal to me my next steps. I needed a sign, like on a billboard, as it was not obvious for me. In the beginning, I would ask my mother to pray for me and this journey, but my mother was still very old school with her thinking. She would give me her usual, "Girl you have a good job, you better stay focused and keep doing well at work. They love you there. Don't mess up and lose that good job talking about scrapbooking and running. You run too much anyway. You need to start dating again." As I took long sighs, I had to remember she loved me and that there were some things I couldn't share with my mother.

Although, my mother was my #1 cheerleader, she was still very conservative and not much of a risk taker. I embodied the same traits, so I needed to be careful with my conversations, or I would talk myself out of exploration. I also had to be careful with which friends I talked to as well. I found some would ask me, "How will you make money scrapbooking. Will that support you?" These conversations created more doubt and confusion, so I learned to limit them. I learned to be my own motivator and cheerleader.

Imagine the possibilities

In the early part of 2016, I was promoted to Director of Sales and my son was accepted into veterinarian school. I couldn't be more excited about our successes. Our lives weren't perfect, but we were definitely thriving. But even in all of our successes something was still missing and I was still searching. During that time, I was surfing Facebook and a fellow runner posted a video, so I decided to listen. She talked about a book launch by one of her friends, called *The Courageous Life*. I decided at that moment, I would purchase the book right away so that I could read it on my plane ride to Canada for work a few days later. It was an easy and great read and I felt excited about the possibility of living a courageous life. A few weeks later, I was shopping in my favorite craft store and whom do I see? It was Melissa Nixon, author of *The Courageous Life*.

I approached her and we began to chat. She told me about her book signing in South Charlotte, scheduled for the next day. I went to the book signing and was energized about her story and the book. Melissa asked her guests several questions, but one question stuck in my head. She asked, "What would you do, if you weren't afraid"? This question was so familiar to me. It was the same question; my late husband would ask. It stirred up feelings in me that I couldn't ignore. God was sending me the billboard I needed to move. My brain started turning and I had so many wonderful business ideas in my head that I had talked myself out of before. Now, they had risen from the dead. I started to jot them down on paper. This could be exciting. I asked myself, "will this be another false start on discovering my purpose in life or will this be my turning point?" I continued to pray for clarity and focus. In my spirit, I felt this was the start of something amazing.

The rug is pulled from beneath

As I was finishing a five-mile run with my running partner on Thursday, December 1, 2016, I saw several missed calls from my mom's best friend. *This can't be good,* I thought, so I called her immediately. I received the news that my mom had a heart attack and had passed away. *God, where are you?* The rug had been pulled from beneath my feet and I was flat on my face crying, yet again. Not only had I lost my husband, but also lost both parents within nine months during the same year. How strong do I have to be? My mom was my rock, my #1 cheerleader, my prayer warrior, the wind beneath my wings, and the person who would ride to the ends of earth with me. Although, I know she's in heaven, I want her here on earth beside me!

I started to replay all of the conversations with her in my head, especially our last conversation. I was in Detroit, Michigan in October for a half marathon, so I was able to see her and spend the weekend at home with her. She fussed about my running pants, as she said they were too tight. She asked how many races I had before I hit the fifty- mark, as she was trying to keep up with them. Although she said I ran too much, she was quietly bragging about how many I ran to her friends. She was so proud of her only grandson and was beaming with joy. She mentioned talking to him on the phone and his study partners were in the back laughing at their conversation. She said she couldn't wait to have the first doctor in the family. Laying my mom and dad to rest in 2016 had to be one of the hardest years in my life. My promise to my mom and dad in heaven is to continue to make them proud of me and to live my best life. There are still days I feel like an adult orphan.

A decision to LIVE

January 2017. It's a New Year and I'm determined to live with no regrets and without FEAR. Vivian Tucker raised a strong woman. I've decided to honor my mother with being the "ROCKSTAR" that she told me I was daily. No crawling under a rock this time around. In 2017, I'm kicking butt and taking names at work and I'm ready to leave my comfort zone to discover my purpose. The year started off with a note I wrote to myself at *The Courageous Life Brunch* in October 2016. Melissa Nixon had the participants write a note and then put it in a self-addressed envelope. To be honest, I actually forgot I did the exercise. When I checked the mailbox and saw my own handwriting, it kind of freaked me out for a moment. That note reminded me of the promises I made myself to be diligent with living life intently and focused.

It was no coincidence that Melissa Nixon contacted me that spring to ask if there was any way she could help me as a Business & Leadership coach. Initially, I was thinking, I've done this before so I might pass. I talked with my best friend that night and she reminded me to *invest* in myself. She reminded me how I would blow that money on something else, which did not have a return. I gave it some thought and sent Melissa an email within twenty-four hours and said "YES – I'm ready to move forward." I had several business ideas I wanted to review and narrow down for further exploration, so I got busy reviewing them. Although I didn't know what idea I would move forward with for sure, I did know that my purpose was to CREATE and INSPIRE. Never had I been clearer in my vision for my life. Although, I think my mother is in heaven probably asking for a pass to come to earth and whisper in my ear, "I'm going for it!"

Coaching calls

My coaching calls with Melissa were awesome. I was prepared for every call and Melissa kept me on task and focused. Having an accountability partner was key in meeting deadlines and moving forward. Although I had several ideas to review, I narrowed it down to one idea that felt right. My idea was to create cards that would inspire, encourage, and celebrate health and fitness achievements. This idea married my love for paper and running. This idea resurfaced several times in my head and heart over the past five years and it spoke to who I am and what I believe in. I'm excited, I'm ready, and I want to explore the possibility in depth. Melissa's calls helped me to develop a strategy to explore and launch, while working full-time in Corporate America. This felt right for me. Things were going well at work and I was not trying to quit my job, just yet. I was so excited about where this was headed.

Although excited, I had a lot of work to do. Launching a greeting card business during a time where social media was at an all-time high, and human connection was now via text and post messages, I had to take this trend into consideration. I asked myself, "although I buy and make cards, is the greeting card industry shrinking? Hallmark stores are closing, the cost of stamps is going up and I'm literally trying to bring snail mail back to life. Who does that?" It didn't make a lot of sense in my head, but I thought to myself, "there are times when matters of the heart doesn't make a lot of sense." I spent weeks reviewing the industry, types of cards, card occasions, cost of cards, packaging, and paper. It's now time to bring this business to life. Now is the time!

Dealing with FEAR and self-sabotage

January 2018, the exploration continued and fear crept in. Will people like my cards? My vision for the cards is changing and evolving, do I need more time? Can I do this? I started extending the launch date further out based upon fear. I changed my logo twice, as it didn't feel right. I started to ask friends for their opinions, which led me to questioning my direction. I got overwhelmed with marketing on social media. Melissa took the time to get me back on track. She reminded me that the same Kimberly Tucker Hall that kicks butt at work is the same entrepreneur launching a business. Mind you, I had just won the *President's Award* at my job for the Top Salesperson in the company for the year before. Now I'm questioning if I can execute. She reminded me of all the small wins I'd made in securing retail space before launch and convinced me to start small with the launch.

I began to regain my confidence and was ready to launch my business. I can and will do this. Long nights working on the business plan, evenings working with designers, researching other card companies, competitive shops, business strategy, website development, supplier review, missed outings with friends, little sleep, and marathon training, all while working a full-time corporate job. I felt like Superwoman. Let's Do This! Nothing worth having is ever easy and I'm ready for the challenge. Everything was fine and dandy until Melissa said I needed to do Facebook live to discuss the upcoming launch. That was a deer in headlight moment for me. I didn't want to be one of those people I frowned upon always going live on Facebook. Don't they have something better to do? I told Melissa I would do it by a certain date, but I didn't. I told her my landing page wasn't ready and that was critical.

Quietly, I was happy it wasn't ready. Actually, I hadn't given my cousin the information to finish it. Announcing this to the world meant that it was real. It meant no turning back. I asked myself, "Am I ready?" I knew a Facebook live had to be done, but it had to be done when *I* was ready and comfortable. I'm at my best when I'm in the zone, right before a race. That was it! I had to go live right before a race and that's what I did. I went live on Facebook to announce to the world that I was launching a greeting card business and bringing snail mail back, right before half marathon #43. I felt good. I told the world about the upcoming birth of my idea (my baby).

Now that I announced the launch into the atmosphere, I had to ultimately finalize my card collection with my designers. How does a creative person make her thoughts come to life? To be honest, I'm still learning. It's like organized chaos in my head. There are some days I question my creativity and my ability to articulate the visual aspects of what I want people to feel. I have thoughts of paradigm shifts, transformations, and mental toughness. I know the feeling I want the person to have reading and seeing a *Sole Inspired* card. I also know the sentiment behind the message, but how I convey it to a designer has been an area that I need improvement.

I've attempted to do this through stock photography, whether free, purchased, or my own design, and also through visualization of drawings. If someone can connect with a photo and imagine themselves in it, then I've jumpstarted the visualization process and my words can begin to manifest hope, love, and courage. For cards without photography, know I've driven several graphic designers crazy and I'm sure they probably don't' want to see my name in an email or on a cell phone again. lol. I'm still finding my groove with designing my cards. In 2019, I've decided to take classes in graphic design to further bring my visions to life, with limitless changes and updates until it's perfect.

Sole Inspired birthed

To think that I was able to birth an idea and launch it, still blows my mind. *Sole Inspired* is definitely my baby and I continue to marvel over my courageous move to launch a business, while working full-time. Delivering hope, love, and courage…one card at a time is the core to its existence. People are excited to receive courage in a card, praise on paper, or a nudge in a note. For those who don't have the time to send a card to a loved one or a friend, *Sole Inspired* gladly writes messages, places a stamp on the envelope and sends it out for our customers. I want to inspire, encourage, and motivate everyone I come in contact with. In a world where there is a lot of turmoil and anxiety from politics, I take joy in the simple meaning of making someone smile. Tomorrow is not promised and every person that we can touch and inspire melts my heart.

The sleepless nights were so worth it. *Sole Inspired* is more than a card company. *Sole Inspired* speaks to the unique journey that we've all gone through in our life, as no one can walk in your shoes. *Sole Inspired* speaks to that indomitable spirit to beat the odds and to never give up. Take a moment and think about your fingerprint. Your fingerprint is unique to you; it's your identifier, as no one else has your fingerprint. Your soles are unique to your journey, as no-one truly understands or has been through what you've been through. You may be in the trenches as you read this, but you will come out on the other side.

Looking ahead

I founded *Sole Inspired* because I felt a need to inspire, encourage, and motivate others in life and in their health and fitness journey. To be honest, when I developed these cards, it was based on the encouragement that *I* needed. Every day, both in running and in daily life, I would tell myself, "don't give up, Kim! You got this! Keep going!" There was something about reading my journal and writing down encouraging words, affirmations, and favorite quotes that set my soul on fire. The days that I felt defeated or discouraged, I would reach for my toolbox of courage on paper. There were some phrases I would read over and over again, as they gave me life and a renewed focus. Some of my favorite phrases: "I choose to be unstoppable, my mind body and spirit are strong, you are capable of amazing things," and my all-time favorite, "act in spite of fear." Act in spite of fear was something that I would read over and over. It reminded me that it's okay to be scared, but sometimes you have to move scared. If words on paper gave me hope, I was sure it could help others as well.

Before our six-month anniversary our cards were already in four retail locations and new products had been added to our product line. Not bad for a woman who did not know her purpose and wondered if she would ever find passion and creativity beyond numbers. The power of connection, paper, and human interaction is not lost in the ages of social media. Our base is paper products, but as we move ahead and grow, our focus will be on delivering hope, love, and courage in all things we do and provide.

I am excited about the wonderful projects ahead. Soon we will be releasing featured Sole Inspirers. Sole Inspirers are people whose character, strength and mental toughness have helped them forge through triumph and victory. *Sole Inspired* will also partner with other organizations and businesses, developing customized cards that provide inspiration and encouragement to their customers. *Sole Inspired* gift boxes and calendars are all items to be released in the near future.

Lessons Learned

My corporate job was my main priority and there were times that I had to let the "analysis paralysis" fall to the wayside, as I no longer was afforded the luxury of over-analyzing everything. When I look back on the launch, it was a good thing that I did it afraid. Fear can sometimes paralyze you, cause you to delay, and sometimes give in or cancel. What I've learned about myself over the years is that my work ethic is always one of excellence, but my desire to strive for perfection is unrealistic. As you know, there is no such thing as perfection. If I waited to launch the cards when I had the perfect graphic designer or the perfect business plan, I would still be reworking everything time and time again.

Sometimes you have to keep your ideas to yourself and not ask for others opinions. Everyone will not understand your vision and your grind. If you aren't strong enough to handle it, others opinions can create uncertainty and fear about your decisions.

I've learned that it's okay to pivot and change direction, as needed. What you launch does not have to be the "end all be all."

Probing questions for you to consider when working a 9-to-5:

1. What would you do as a career, if money were not a factor or consideration? What would your dream job look like?

2. What is holding you back from exploring this possibility?

3. What sets your soul on fire? Will you look back years from now and regret not fueling this fire?

4. For those of you who are known as a top achiever and make things happen, day in and day out at work, do you show up in that capacity for yourself? What would it look like if you did?

5. When will you make the time to explore other opportunities that keep you up at night or are ingrained in your spirit?

God's Promises

Be anxious for nothing, but in everything by prayer and supplication, with thanksgiving, let your requests be made known to God and the peace of God, which surpasses all understanding, will guard your hearts and minds through Christ Jesus. **Philippians 4:6-8 (NIV)**

I lift up my eyes to the mountains – where does my help come from? My help comes from the Lord, the Maker of heaven and earth. **Psalm 121:1-2 (NIV)**

Prayer

Father, I thank you for every woman working a 9-to-5 right now who either feels called to something different or something more. I pray that she would show up for herself and the dreams you have placed inside of her as she does for her job and others. Remind her that she is just as gifted and talented to live out her God-Sized dream as she is in her full-time career. I pray where she has doubts and insecurities that you replace them with trust and faith. Where her time seems limited, that you would multiply it.

Remind her of who she is and more importantly, remind her of who You are. That You have called her to great things. You have not called her to a life of mediocrity. You have not called her to a life of being average, but You have called her to a life of abundance. That you will not let her fail and that You have not given her a dream that You cannot fulfill. That You have gone even beyond her today into her future and You're there waiting. You're there waiting to supply all her needs. You're there waiting to help with the resources. You're there waiting on her. Thank You for her life, her career, and her dreams, in Jesus' name we pray, amen.

Insert your prayer and/or affirmations if you are building your dream while working your 9-to-5:

Chapter 6

Achieving Your Dream at
Any Age

Joan Turley

Get on the ride

I wanted to be brave...I really did. But truth be told, I was scared to death. I didn't think I could take another step. I swear, I could barely breathe. I thought I was going to pass out right then and there on that old rickety wooden platform. My knees were knocking so hard—they bout' buckled right out from under me. If I could have, I would have turned tail and ran like a scalded dog, but my daddy had a hold of my tiny hand, white knuckles and all, and he wasn't about to turn loose of me or let me run away in fear—like some old scaredy-cat.

So, we slid into the worn-out red leather two-seater bench with a steel bar locked across our laps, and before I could even scream, "get me off of this thing" the words got stuck in my throat and I could not spit them out for the life of me. I was petrified. There was no turning back. Up, up, up, higher and higher we climbed and then suddenly we plummeted down a perilous white mountain at the speed of light. Over and over again we rose and fell to the thrills and chills of the old wooden roller-coaster...the Zypher of New Orleans. Why that old roller-coaster was so timeworn my daddy rode it when he was nothing but knee-high to a bullfrog.

I was but a wisp of a girl when my daddy took me on that first roller-coaster ride. Never before had I tasted such dread and delight all in one breath-taking moment. Fear and joy bound together in one magnificent flash of a ride. And then it was over—faster than we could have ever imagined. Before the ride, I was scared to death; after the ride, I knew that I had nothing to fear because my daddy had an unshakable hold on me. With every twist and every turn, with every rise and every fall—my daddy held me safe within his arms. Oh, what a ride we shared—it was glorious!

Isn't that just like life? There are highs and there are lows but through it all we are held securely by a God who will never let us go. We are never alone, even in those scary moments. We are held. Now that I am older, looking back over years of tears and fears, this is what I have come to know, those highs and lows, those moments of great happiness and deep heartbreak and everything in between—those are the moments that give us our victory stories—real stories worth telling and retelling around the campfires of our lives. Those are the truest of stories we will ever tell, those are the stories that will eternally impact the lives of those we love the most. Today, my words of encouragement to you are, "get on the ride!" You are held by the grip and grace of God and He will not abandon you! Do not let fear keep you from getting on the ride, because God is always and forever by your side. He's got you from here to eternity. So get on the ride because when it's all said and done—it's all going be over quicker than you can imagine. Trust Him.

Lean in close and listen to me—I know it can be scary—I know all about those fears that are pounding on your front door. For more years than I care to remember, I dreamed of writing a book. The dream never left me. It swirled inside my soul like an ache in the bones that never goes away. Truth be told, it would be thirty years before I found the courage to slam the door on fear and pursue that dream of writing my first book. No sooner had I written and published the book, there came "fear" pounding on my door once more. Fear said, "So you wrote the book—big deal! You waited too long. No one is going to read your book; because, you're just a nobody and no one even knows your name. So, just who do you think you are? Your book is not going to make an ounce of difference?"

Fear comes to us all. Come on now—you know what I'm talking about. Here is one I'm real familiar with... "I can't go and start that now...because I'm too old." Or, how about this one, "Do you know how many years I've worked that job—I've been passed over so many times I've lost count. I can't go and start all over now." How about this one,

"I've lived my whole life in this city. I can't just up and move to the other side of the world." Oh yes you can...if God says so!

But typically, this is what happens; we let our fears become self-limiting beliefs that we embrace. And along the way, those self-limiting beliefs start to dictate what we think we can and cannot do. Even worse, we let those self-limiting beliefs put us in a box. Like, "all I am is a wife, all I am is mom, all I am is a grandmother, or all I am is a friend." Now let me be clear, those are all wonderful gifts from God—gifts that absolutely melt our hearts with love. But if we're honest, there's a stirring in our souls for something more.

There's a holy discontent pulling on our heartstrings. Because, the truth of the matter is this; God has whispered in the still of the night, "O Sweet child of mine, I have given you spheres of influence and created you to be a difference maker in the lives of those who live within your circles of impact. Daughter, don't you know—I've made you to shine for my glory? I have so much more for you! And, if you trust me, I will take you places and show you things you've never seen before. I will give to you divine assignments. In fact, the things that you have dreamed about for years are the dreams I placed within your heart."

I've got this feeling that you've heard His whisper too. I'm betting there are longings in your heart that only God can fulfill. And sometimes, the longings and the waiting are painful. I know that. I've been there too. But hold on dear friend, God is not finished with you yet. Hear me out—once I was young and now I am old(er) and I have walked some roads with God. I've fallen in more potholes than you could possibly imagine! But, in spite of my fallings and failings, I have seen His faithfulness and I've got a few stories to tell—stories that just might cause your heart to find the "get-up-and-go" you need to pursue your God-Sized dream. What do you say? Are you ready to get on the ride? I hope so; because, my prayer for you is that you will slay those self-limiting beliefs right here and now and embrace your God-Sized dreams.

Pulling up stakes

*"In God's Kingdom — growing older means a
flourishing that gets sweeter and sweeter, fuller and
fuller, and more and more of His precious spirit poured
out upon our lives."*

Maybe I've watched one too many "happily ever after" movies. I don't know. But at any rate, the picture I had in my head of what one's "golden years" were supposed to look like doesn't match the life I'm living now—not one tiny little bit! Somehow, I had gotten it into my head that surely there would come a day where we would cross some invisible line (this side of heaven) and we'd never have to stand in faith again for a God-Sized miracle. Now...isn't that ridiculous? But, right or wrong, that's what I had subconsciously come to believe. So, imagine my surprise when everything fell apart.

Let me explain. Life was good in Texas. My husband had a great job— a job he'd held for twenty-two years. I had a job I dearly loved—my favorite job ever! We were growing older and life looked grand. But, 2015 turned everything on its head. The company I worked for closed its doors and suddenly I was jobless. But it wasn't just that I was jobless—it was more than that. In our heart of hearts and deep within our spirits—we knew it was time for a colossal change. It was time to close a significant chapter, to turn the page and start a new adventure. But I'd be less than honest if I didn't tell you that I was scared to death. Some days—I still am.

My husband and I had prayed for many years that someday God would move us to Tennessee. Although our feet were planted in Texas our hearts were in Nashville with the family whose company we craved. We had no idea how God would fulfill our deepest longing and we certainly never imagined that it would be the biggest faith-stretching adventure of our lives. I mean who in their right mind would venture off into the wild blue yonder, when they are well past their prime and on the brink of enjoying those blissful golden years? I certainly never imagined in a million years that God would call us to an "Abraham Adventure" in the last quarter of our lives. All I can say is "I'm glad we didn't know how hard the journey would be; because, if we had known how much our faith would be stretched, we might not have found the courage to follow Him into the glorious unknown. What memory-making impactful moments we would have missed!

So, we made the big move. Like Abraham of old, we pulled up our stakes, packed our bags and said goodbye to thirty years of beautiful friendships and hello to a brand-new life a thousand miles away—far from the beautiful home we had loved so well. Our future was clear as mud. The only comforting thing was the reassurance that at least my husband had a job. And that's when the faith adventure really began. His company made the decision to disallow him to work remotely and within six months we were both jobless! This was definitely not what I had bargained for—not what I had envisioned. I seriously began to question every decision that we had ever made. I wondered if we had taken a wrong turn. Had we missed God? Everything we had put before Him in prayer, He had confirmed. He had clearly given us a green light. There were so many signs and confirmations that He was leading us to follow Him on this new adventure, but, at this stage on the journey, it sure felt like the rug had just been pulled out from under us.

I did not understand what was happening. All I knew was that I was scared—more scared than I have ever been. Nonetheless, in my fear I began to hear God whisper, "Go look at Abraham's journey. Open up the Word—take a fresh look at his journey. Sweet child, I know your heart. You have prayed for a God-Sized story, a story that will bring me great glory—go back and look again at the life of Abraham." So, I opened the pages to a very familiar story, only this time I saw something that I had not noticed before. How had I never noticed that when God told Abraham to pull up his tent pegs and go.... what God actually said, was "Go to a land that *I will show you*"—not that I have shown you—but that I will show you. The scripture says, "And Abraham went...not knowing where he was going." Now I knew that Abraham went not knowing where he was going, but I had never picked up on the fact that God had said to Abraham "go to a land that I **will** show you."

God was inferring that Abraham's journey would be an unfolding journey, a journey taken one step at time. It would only be revealed as he walked with God one day at a time. Additionally, God would give Abraham a magnificent promise; he and his barren wife, Sarah, would finally have a child. But, unbeknownst to Abraham and Sarah—there would be a divine delay in the fulfillment of that promise. I'm talking decades of delay. God would wait to fulfill that promise until there was no way humanly possible for the promise to be fulfilled.

Think about this—it is not until we come to the end of ourselves that God can receive the glory. A glory that only God deserves. So, God would wait to bring the promised son to Abraham and Sarah until their bodies were old and just about worn out. And we see this pattern repeated over and over again in Scripture. He gives Joseph a dream, but fails to mention "oh by the way—you're going to go through some really hard times, like being sold into slavery, then thrown into prison for a crime you didn't commit, before this dream comes to pass. But I will make something beautiful out of your life—I promise." He anoints David as King, but it will be years before David rules and reigns over the house of Israel. He will be hunted down like a dog—fleeing the vindictive wrath of Saul for many long years. But there will come a day when David ascends to the throne of Israel—just as God declared.

So, I began to understand that God was saying to me, "I'm not about to waste your last quarter...your last season...not one tiny bit! I have spoken and declared in My Word that 'the righteous shall flourish—even in old age they shall bear much fruit.' And so, it shall be with you." I love that God intends for us to flourish until He calls us home. Not only that— look at what He shows us in John chapter two. If you get anything from this chapter, this is what I pray you will remember.

In John chapter two, Jesus turns the water into wine (His first miracle). Now watch this...His mother comes to Him and says, "they've run out of wine," She then turns to the servants and says, "do whatever He tells you to do." Jesus, tells the servants to fill the pots with water. The servants do as Jesus tells them to do and the water is turned to wine.

Now lean in close, because this is powerful. Next thing you know, the master of the wedding celebration says to the host of the wedding, "you have saved the best wine for last. Most people put out the best wine first, but you have saved the best for last." Don't miss this—because it's a picture of what God does for you and for me... as we grow old and walk with Him. When we are young and fall in love… we think we know love. Then, we have children and discover a fierce love like no other. But then, we have grandchildren and that love is indescribable. It is the sweetest most precious love this side of heaven. And that is a perfect picture of what God does for us — as we walk with Him through the years, it gets sweeter and sweeter. Because, He saves the very best for last!

In God's Kingdom growing older means a flourishing that gets sweeter and sweeter, fuller and fuller, and more and more of His precious spirit poured out upon our lives. There is no shrinking back, no diminishing in the spirit, but an ever-deepening communion with a God who saves the very best for the last.

Do you see it now? We are called to walk a faith-filled journey, and the things He calls us to do we cannot do on our own. If we could, it would not be a faith journey. And if it is not a faith journey, then it will never be a journey that impacts the lives of those we love the most. I want good things for my children and for all of those within my circle of influence. I want them to be successful, but more than anything in the world—I want them to know Jesus in an intimate and personal way. I want them to experience the God of the Bible, so that they might know Him as Father and Friend long after I am gone. I imagine that's what you want too.

Red sea moments

If we want the people we love the most to know that the God of the Bible, who lives in us, still does miracles today, we've got to be willing to let God walk us to the Red Sea—to that place where only God can deliver. However, it's never easy to stand on shores of the Red Sea, with the enemy just a hair's breadth away threatening to completely devour us. But, when God comes through, when He does that miracle just for you, that's when you have a God-story that your children and those you love the most will never forget. And I promise you they will be telling those God-stories for generations to come. Those Red Sea Moments will be your legacy stories…if you let Him take you to the Red Sea.

Now, maybe this is the first time you've ever heard someone talk about Red Sea Moments. If it is, then this is what I want you to know; when you stand on the shore of a Red Sea Moment you may be tempted to say, "God, did I miss it? Did I take a wrong turn? What's happening? How are we going to get through this?" I'm here to tell you, it is in the middle of our muddles, when we cannot see a way forward, that God speaks at just the right moment, the waters part and we walk through on dry ground. We make it safely to the other side! And the enemy is destroyed, vanquished, utterly defeated.

I remember my first red sea moment. Years ago, my husband and I had been in full-time ministry. We thought we'd be in that ministry our whole lives. In fact, we never imagined ourselves anywhere else but in that ministry. However, twelve years into the journey, that ministry crumbled due to a moral failure on the part of the leadership and a doctrine of extreme legalism. With barely a penny to our name, my husband and I limped our way back to Texas with two small children and nothing to show for the years we had invested into that ministry. We were busted and broken and starting all over at ground zero. We could scarcely put food on the table. To say that I was shattered and angry at God would be an understatement. My life was in shambles and my faith was hanging on by a thread. I felt like God had been less than faithful—like He had completely forgotten all about us. Where was His provision in our poverty?

One day I was standing in my kitchen, staring at pantry shelves that contained nothing but bread, when I blurted out, "Where's your faithfulness in all this God?" I literally raised my fists to the heavens, and I said, "God, I know that King David said 'I have been young and now I'm old, but I have never seen the righteous forsaken, or his descendants begging bread.' Well we got bread—just bread! Thank you very much!" I am sorry to say that I took it a bit further and got really sarcastic with God because, I said, "And by the way, when you said, 'I know the plans I have for you, plans for welfare...' did you mean I'd be on welfare?" I know—that was really ugly—but that's exactly what I said.

I cannot begin to tell you how grateful I am that He overlooked my ugliness and resentment—that He loved me in spite of how awful I behaved. Because, about two hours later there was a knock on my front door. I opened the door and there stood a woman I had not seen in years. I looked at her and simply said, "Sheryl, what are you doing here?" She looked me square in the eyes and then wagged her finger in my face and said, "God told me to come." Then, she turned around, walked to her van, slid open the door and began bringing in bags and bags of groceries. I mean, my kids jumped up and down like it was Christmas morning. There was peanut butter, strawberries and grapes, milk and eggs and packages of fresh meat. Beautiful life-sustaining food! As she turned to leave, she handed me a one-hundred dollar bill in front of my little ones. Well, needless to say, I bawled like a baby. I pulled my children into my lap and whispered between the sobs, "it pays to serve Jesus...never forget sweet babies of mine that it pays to serve Jesus."

And as the tears subsided this is what my sweet Jesus whispered to me, "Oh Joan, you said more than anything in the world you wanted your children to know that the God of the Bible is the same God today as He was yesterday and He will be tomorrow and that He still does miracles today. Well, they won't know that unless you allow me to take you to the Red Sea. Will you trust me when I walk you to edge of the Red Sea? Because that is where you will get your faith stories to pass down to your children. Oh, won't you let me take you to the Red Sea time and time again?"

The secret to finding your courage to be brave when you are standing on the shores of a Red Sea Moment—waiting for God to deliver—is to make spending time with God a non-negotiable. For me, it is the only way forward. See, there came a time when God said, "You want to walk with me? Well, I want that more than you do. Meet me in the morning. Show up with your Bible, a journal and a cup of coffee, and I will teach you my ways. I will change your life, if you will meet me in the morning." And those who know me best will tell you, "everything changed when she started meeting God in the morning."

Isaiah 55: 10-11 says, "For just as the rain and the snow fall from heaven, and do not return there without saturating the earth and making it germinate and sprout, and providing seed to sow, and food to eat, So my Word that comes from my mouth with not return to me empty, but will accomplish what I please, and I will prosper it and when I send it I will do it." In other words, when we spend time in God's Word, He promises that the time we invest in His Word will become like a seed buried in the ground. His rain from heaven will fall upon that "Word seed" buried in the soil of our lives. That precious seed hidden in the ground will not be able to resist the rain of God. It will surely sprout up and bare much fruit!

When we soak in His good Word and let God do His work in us, as my pastor says, "when we get into the Word, the Word gets into us." God starts to grow His spirit within us and our faith is strengthened to believe God that the impossible will become possible. Make spending time with God a non-negotiable, make it the highest priority in your life and just watch and see what God does in your life when you make His Word preeminent above every other voice in your life. He will give you Red Sea Moments that will take your breath away, bow you down in adoration, and raise you up with shouts of joy as the waters part before a watching world.

He never stops wanting to display His glory through our lives. It doesn't matter how old we are or how long we've walked with the Lord; He will always want to stretch and grow our faith. And why is that? Because, without faith it is impossible to please God. God takes great joy in watching us learn to walk by faith. Just as a daddy delights to behold his toddling baby take those first teetering steps—so Father God delights in our journey of faith, even when we stumble and fall.

Dream fulfilled

Remember when we pulled up stakes after living in Texas for thirty years to relocate to Nashville? Let me go back to our move to Nashville. I know that I left some of you hanging—wondering what happened when the hubby lost his job too. Long story short, God provided a job for my husband. I'll be honest, I couldn't believe it when it happened. I mean who hires a 68-year-old man? That was all I could think about in the waiting season. What crossed my mind a million times a day was, "in this youth obsessed culture, who would hire my snowy-white-headed man?" I mean shame on me! I should have known better. But I confess, my faith was shaking as I stood on the shores of another Red Sea waiting for God to part the waters. And what can I say—but that God never fails to deliver in spite of my quivering faith! He provided a job for my husband and to this day we are bowed down in deepest gratitude for the job He gave my beloved snowy-white-headed man. And this we know it has only been God that has held us steadfastly on this faith-stretching journey. We never imagined we'd be walking through it at this stage of our married life.

Knowing Ken had employment, we settled into our Nashville home and I began to write that book I had dreamed about writing for over thirty years and now I was sixty. Talk about holding on to a dream! Doubts swirled in my head and came as fast as I could write. I could feel the panic rising in my heart every time I picked up the pen to write. Can I just tell you, God sent a flood of encouragement to counteract the fear. There were days that I felt like He was sitting right beside me, whispering in my ear, "Just take the next right step baby girl...don't worry about tomorrow...just take the next right step."

I still can't believe it's real. But I am thrilled to say that by the grace of God my book has been published! Yes! You heard me right and it's available on Amazon. It's called *Sacred Work in Secular Places: Finding Joy in The Workplace—An Invitation to Partner with God in A Beautiful Broken World.* To date it has received more than eighty "five-star" reviews and it was a finalist in the 2018 Author Academy Awards—an award bestowed for literary merit and publishing excellence in the writing and publishing industry. Only God...that's all I can say.... Only God.

I simply wrote about overcoming a serious work-related depression to leading and loving an amazing team of talented individuals. I wrote about finding joy in the workplace. Why? Because every day people get up and go to work, but most people (about 80%) hate their jobs and find themselves longing for more than just a paycheck. Their hearts have grown weary on the daily grind and depression holds them captive. Goodness gracious, I know what that's like. For more years than I care to remember—I was a card-carrying, long-standing, member of "The Eighty-Percent Disengaged and Dissatisfied Club". I was a hater of work and I was miserable.

Since the day I gave my life to Christ, I had only ever dreamed of being in "full time ministry." When that dream shattered, I felt like my life would never amount to anything significant. I mean all I had was "just" a job and I was "just" a worker. I worked that nine-to-five like I was tethered to a ball and chain. I was miserable in the workplace; especially, when I compared myself to friends who were flourishing on the foreign mission field or serving in pastoral roles. Needless to say, I felt like chopped liver! Like everyone else was living the dream except me. I was so unhappy. Yet, in the middle of my misery a divine discontent began to stir wildly in my soul. I didn't understand it. I didn't know what God was doing. But that discontent drove me to my knees and into the Scriptures. And what I discovered in the pages of His Holy Word changed the trajectory of my life forever.

Did you know that God first shows up in Genesis as a worker? He is a worker who loves His work! In fact, after each day of work, He declared, as though He were clapping His hands with joy, "It is good, it is good, it is very good!" That is the first picture we get of God—that He is working and loving His work. And it wasn't hard for me to connect the dots that made me in His image. If God loved work, then I could love work too. We were created to share in His work upon the earth.

In discovering that God loved work, He also began to show me that in His sovereignty He made each of us for a divine purpose. He would call some to foreign fields, some to stand behind pulpits, and others to partner with Him in this beautiful broken world among the masses of the everyday workers. In His eyes, there was no dichotomy between the sacred and the secular. More importantly, I began to sense that He had been preparing me for a work that was yet to come. So, I realized that there was a divine delay. He had a place for me to shine for His glory, but the time had not yet come, because He was still doing a work in me.

As providence would have it, there came a day that I walked into that God-appointed job. Only, I didn't know it. I was clueless. I had no idea that "that job" was the job for which He had been uniquely preparing me to hold for years. I did not know when I first walked through the doors of "that job" that God was going to change the arc of my life. Truth be told, when I walked through those doors, I thought God had made a mistake. Want to know what I really said? I literally stopped in my tracks, looked around and whispered under my breath, "Oh my Lord, you have sent me to Babylon and this is not going to work. Look at me God, lily-white, Southern Baptist, pretty conservative. Look at them, every color of the rainbow—guys and gals, divas, straights and gays, blue- haired biddies, blond-haired bombshells, pink-haired punks and everything in between. They're not like me, this is not going to work." God whispered…rather boldly…and pretty fiercely, "you are so right, they are not like you—they are like me! These people are made in my image and that makes them precious to me; therefore, they need to be precious to you. Love them well, because I am entrusting them into your care."

With that gentle rebuke, an invisible barrier came crashing down. Suddenly it wasn't about my political persuasion or spiritual convictions—it was about loving the people right where they were because they were precious to God—even if they did not know Him. The late Billy Graham said it best when he said, "It is God's job to judge, it is the Holy Spirit's job to convict, and it is my job to love." I felt like God was trying to say to me in the kindest of ways, "get out of the way of the Holy Spirit, you are not Him, you never will be. Leave the convicting work of the Spirit to Me. Your only job is to love them and serve them well. And, when my conviction falls upon them, if you have prayed for them and loved them well, then they will know that they can count on you to show them how to walk with Me." And that is how I discovered joy in the workplace—and the sweetest days I've ever known.

That "job" of learning to lead with love, a people who were precious to God, lead me to where I am today—a motivational speaker, author and ghostwriter, and a heart-driven leadership coach. But it did not happen overnight. I held that God-appointed job for almost ten years. And I am here telling you, I am more convinced than ever that God does not waste one day of our life experiences!

And this is what I want to say to you. I don't know where you are on your journey with God. Maybe you feel like you're in a dead-end situation or stuck in a divine delay with no end in sight. I've walked long enough with God to know that if He can do it for me, He most certainly will do it for you. In the middle of your muddles, He can speak to someone on your behalf to help you carry the load—just like He did for me when He delivered groceries to my doorstep. I didn't know how we could put food on the table. He knows what you're going through. He knows your thoughts, He knows your beliefs, He knows what financial need you have. He knows. And He will not fail you.

So how about it? Are you ready to embrace your God-Sized dream at any age? I hope so. Now, I confess, that I do not know where you are on your journey with God, nor your age or the obstacles that lay before you. But, if perhaps, you are of a certain age, where your hair's gone gray, and there's no hiding the wrinkles around your eyes, and people say "yes ma'am" and "no ma'am" as a sign of respect, well I've got good news for you! This ain't no time for shrinking back or giving up. Till you take that dying last breath, there's a work for you to do. A dream still yet to be fulfilled.

So, I'll ask you one last time. Do you truly, madly, deeply believe that age is not a factor when it comes to embracing your God-Sized dream? And just in case you need an extra ounce of courage, take a look at the words of Caleb, found written in the book of Joshua. "Here I am today, eighty-five years old. I am still as strong today as I was the day Moses sent me out. My strength for battle and for daily tasks is now as it was then. (Joshua 14:10b-11) (CSB). I'm claiming that verse over my life. How about you? And if that's not enough, if you still need more, Psalms 92:14 boldly declares that "Even in old age they will still produce fruit; they will remain vital and green." (NLT) That is a promise that you can take to the bank.

It's time to get on the ride and trust your life to the One who will never let you go. I promise, with every high and every low, it will be the most glorious, scariest, thrillingest ride ever. A ride with no regrets. And when at last He calls you home, you shall say with all your heart, to those you love the most, "The ride, oh the ride, it was the most glorious thing I've ever done. I wish I could do all again. But, until then, I'll be waiting for you on the other side. Praying, that you too will get on the ride and follow Him all the days of your life."

Lessons Learned

When I look back over my journey, if I could change anything it would be that I would trust more and stress less. I would not fret or worry about the outcome of difficult situations. Honestly, I often scratch my head and wonder why I have stressed so much and fretted myself into a frenzied mess. Because, looking back, I can clearly see the evidence that God has never once failed me. He has proved to be more than faithful.

What's next?

As I look ahead this is what I know. He's not finished with me yet. These remaining days, however long they may be, will surely be the best days ever. He saves the best for last because that's what He has promised. So, I'm not backing down or shying away from all that He has for me. Oh, to be sure, there will come a day that God will call me home and with all my heart I know that it will not be a fearful journey at all. When that day comes, He will take me by the hand and say, "See, I promised you that I would be with you every single day of your life. And I am with you even now." And with this knowledge there is an ever-growing peace that to know God is the greatest joy of all and truthfully, all that I have known is but a shadow of what I will know when I am safely on the other side. Until then, I will follow Him with all my heart.

Probing questions for you to consider your dream at any age:

1. What goals and dreams do you have that you have allowed negative thoughts about your age get in the way?

2. What do you think Jesus would say about your age and the dream that you have?

3. Write down 2 - 3 role models of women your age (who has accomplished a similar dream.

4. What next step can you take after reading my story and theirs?

God's Promises

The Lord himself goes before you and will be with you; he will never leave you nor forsake you. Do not be afraid; do not be discouraged." **Deuteronomy 31:8 (NIV)**

Have I not commanded you? Be strong and courageous. Do not be afraid; do not be discouraged, for the Lord your God will be with you wherever you go. **Joshua 1:9 (NIV)**

Cast your cares on the Lord and he will sustain you he will never let the righteous be shaken. **Psalm 55:22 (NIV)**

For no matter how many promises God has made, they are "Yes" in Christ. And so through him the "Amen" is spoken by us to the glory of God. **2 Corinthians 1:20 (NIV)**

What, then, shall we say in response to these things? If God is for us, who can be against us? **Romans 8:31 (NIV)**

Prayer

Heavenly Father, I pray for every woman reading this book especially for those that feel they are too young, too old, or have to wait until a certain age to do what you have called her to do.

I pray for every woman who has heard the pounding of fear on her front door and the whispered lies of the enemy. Today, may she find the courage to live her bravest, boldest life ever—for your glory. Cause your Word to take root in her soul and grow into a promise fulfilled. Oh Lord, give her glorious Red Sea Moments that will astound the world at the might and wonder of her God. And may all who know her marvel at the work that you are doing in and through her life.

Let her know her true worth and significance. Oh God, I can just imagine as You were fashioning her, knitting her together in her mother's womb, then pouring gifts, talents and abilities into her being, then stepping back and declaring with joy, "Oh I can't wait to see how she is going to use these gifts for my glory." Lord, I pray tonight that she would believe with all of her might, that You want good things for her and that You will use her life in amazing ways through every season and all of her days.

We're told in the book of Ephesians that before the foundation of the world, you prepared good works for us to do. May she find those beautiful good works that You have prepared for her and take great joy in knowing not only whose she is but who she is. Help her to discover her purpose. Lord, for the woman that is reading this passage—may she dream big dreams and have a heart to run hard after You.

I pray that just as you sent people to me when I was at a low point, that you will send people to her whenever she is in need of encouragement. As You have sent people to speak hope to me, may you do that for her. Send her people that will spur her on to love and good works. Send her people that will be like that armor bearer was to Jonathan, who when

Jonathan said "this is what I want to do," the armor bearer said to Jonathan, "whatever's in your heart to do, go do it, I'm with you. I will stand with you." That is my prayer for the women who read this book. May they be encouraged to dream big dreams, to pray bold prayers. And may we as women have the heart and the will to support one another in every good endeavor...for the glory of God.

I pray for every reader, wherever they may be in the world and thank You for doing something amazing in all of their lives.

In Jesus's name.

Amen.

Insert your own prayer and/or affirmation about pursuing your dream at any age:

Chapter 7

Overcoming Distractions

Cheryl Riley

Life sets us up! Home, work, church, children, and spouses, you name it we are pulled at every turn. These common interactions, along with the unexpected events that present themselves, can cause one to get off track and to lose focus. There are times when even the good things in life can cause us to be counterproductive and work against the goals we have set for ourselves. As I ponder my journey, I have observed how life's occurrences and my responses to them have resulted in the fulfillment, or lack of fulfillment of my dreams and divine purposes.

I entered college in the mid-eighties with aspirations of becoming a computer analyst (i.e., make big money). I majored in Mathematics with a concentration in Computer Science and forged ahead. A year and a half later, I found myself pregnant and having to make a major life decision. I'm not proud to say that I teetered on what that decision ought to be. Prior to arriving at college, I had been instructed by a member of my church, as she gifted me with items for my dorm, not to allow my educational journey to be interrupted. We all knew exactly what she meant. Yet, here I was facing that very situation. This was a pivotal moment in my life. I was an honor student who was very involved in the college life. I was excited about all the great things that were occurring and lie ahead. This situation could potentially sideline me. I was reminded of that encounter with the church member and somehow something in me ignited. I began having conversations with myself, "This circumstance will not deter me from my goal. I will receive my degree and it will be completed in four years."

I remained true to my word and gave birth to my daughter in November and returned to school two weeks later. I finished the semester, the year, and graduated in the Spring of the following year with a Mathematics Degree. During this period, I worked three jobs, received several additional scholarships to fund my education, completed a paid internship, and was offered a job opportunity upon graduation. So it appeared that I had it all together. I was a go-getter. Self-motivated, goal-focused, and proactively pressing toward my goals. From the outside, no one would ever think that I had an issue fulfilling my purpose. I had a proven track record that whatever I put my mind to, I could accomplish. Yet it took years of stops and starts to help me find my purpose. Enter distractions. I was overwhelmed with life, people, and stuff that consumed me.

A distraction is a thing that prevents one from giving their full attention to something else. It is a diversion or recreation, an extreme agitation of the mind or emotions. Like me, I am sure you have experienced each version as defined. Life had presented those things that pulled my attention from what needed to be accomplished. There have been self-inflicted diversions; a television show, social media, or time with others. Although none of these activities are necessarily a *bad* thing, it was not always the right *time* for it. Then there are thoughts and encounters that plant seeds of uncertainty, sadness, or worry that begin to crowd your mind and take you on side journeys that detour your confidence and distort your opinion of yourself. Too much time spent here is unsafe, unproductive, and dangerous to your purpose and the fulfillment of your God-Sized dream.

It doesn't matter how long it takes

I received my undergraduate degree in May of 1989. My initial aspiration was to go directly to graduate school and obtain my Master's in Computer Science. However, while my daughter being born during my junior year in college was a blessing, it was not the plan we had. Instead of heading off to the university we headed down the aisle in the fall of '89. In February of 1990 I became pregnant with our second child and first son. And again, in 1992 with another son. We were too busy doing other things as you can see. Yet, in August of 1993, I began my master's pursuit by taking a course in the fall and another in the spring of 1994.

At that time, my husband was working retail and had a crazy schedule that required him to work twelve-hour days either early in the morning or late at night. Our children were all under the age of eight and someone had to be home for them, so I took my first break. I began again in 1997 returning to the same university and took another course where I actually struggled. As a result, I was a bit disheartened with the course outcome and took another break that lasted for seven years.

In 2004, I began again, but at a different university. Due to the time lapse, I lost the credits gained at the initial institution. I enrolled and completed courses during the spring and summer semesters, then, life happened yet again. I was working a second job, facilitating workshops two to three weekends a month, all while preparing for our daughter's graduation and college entrance. My nephew was living with us at the time, and all four of the children were heavily involved in various activities. There was so much going on. Enter break number three.

So, let me stop for moment and interject here. Not everything is a distraction. Sometimes it is about timing. A delay is not a "no," it may just mean not right now. Life happens. Not only does it happen, it can sideline our aspirations. This is what break three was; my dream had to be sidelined periodically since I had four teenagers immersed in a myriad of activities. I sacrificed my dreams for a season. It was not my time. Well, as I stated earlier, they all made it through the trials of adolescence and matriculated to college. During our youngest son's junior year in high school, he made a profound statement as he started to exit the car. I don't remember the circumstances surrounding the statement, where we were coming from or if we had even been discussing the subject, but as we got out the car, he exclaimed, "Mama, i'mma need you to get that masters." Neither he nor I knew at the time that this was perfect timing because history was about to repeat itself. Had I not returned to the second university during that semester, I would have lost my credits yet again. I finished the required courses needed to receive my teaching certification. Funny, I had been teaching mathematics for twenty-one years and although I believed I was doing a good job, my respect for the craft pushed me to obtain my professional credentials.

On the final night of class, as our professor conducted exit interviews, she questioned my reasoning for pursuing my Masters of Arts in Teaching (MAT). She said, "You have been doing this for twenty plus years, you are a master teacher." She continued by sharing information on a new program at yet another university. They were beginning their first cohort for Administrators where individuals could earn a degree in Executive Leadership Studies along with a Principal Certification. Well, I never wanted to be a teacher though I now knew that was what I was called to be. I also KNEW I did not want to be an administrator. I witnessed the responsibilities of the job with my mentor and I did not want that. I had that conversation with my professor on Thursday. The following Monday my principal entered our morning meeting with a hot pink piece of paper detailing a new Administrator's Program at a local university. Yes, you guessed it, the exact program my professor had shared with me.

Well, as we all know God knows how to get us to our place in Him. "For I know the plans I have for you," declares the LORD, "plans to prosper you and not to harm you, plans to give you hope and a future." Jeremiah 29:11(NIV) This new program would take five semesters, less time than at my current school due to required prerequisite courses. Wow, God is good! The time that appeared to have been a distraction was all a part of His plan. As I aligned myself to His timing, He perfected the path. I graduated and ended up with two new positions that I did not seek.

My time standing before and beside students has not always been smooth sailing; in fact, I have attempted to leave on several occasions. But each time my Heavenly Father reminded me that He has called me to this space. I have been called to these children to assist them in identifying and becoming who God has called them to be. However, teaching is work. Listen to what James says about teaching:

Not many [of you] should become teachers
[serving in an official teaching capacity],
My brothers and sisters, for you know that we
[who are teachers] will be judged by a higher standard
[because we have assumed greater accountability
and more condemnation if we teach incorrectly].
James 3:1 (AMP)

Wow, this is so true. Teachers are strapped with the responsibility of developing the personnel for all professions, yet they often feel undercompensated, overextended, overwhelmed, and pulled in every direction. Yet, it is one of the greatest honors and most rewarding things one could ever do. So, how do we keep them encouraged and in the classroom?

I have learned that teachers and administrators, including myself, need to be poured back into. Shortly after receiving my Masters, I was nominated and recognized as one of the top twenty-five teachers by an organization in our local area. The mission of this organization was to identify and retain good teachers in our classrooms. This was indeed an honor. It brought to light the ongoing need to encourage, celebrate, and appreciate educators for their work and commitment to our children. Our induction into the program took place over four days where we received inspiring professional development workshops, massages, automobiles were detailed, palettes satisfied, and long-lasting relationships were established. The perks continued afterwards, offering ongoing personal development, cultural, and entertainment outings as well as annual alumni fellowships and gatherings. It is opportunities like this that have kept me fueled and given me the ideas to pour back into my own teachers throughout the years.

My God-Sized Dream

For twenty years My God-Sized dream has been to write a book. The initial plan was to write a book of lessons learned from rearing our three children. People who knew our family would often comment on their accomplishments and would commend us for it. Little did they know we were not smart enough to do that on our own. We simply had sense enough to submit to and trust God and rely on His wisdom to guide and rear them in the fear and admonition of the Lord. We allowed God to direct us and took to heart His mandate to produce a godly generation. Now, our three are by no means perfect, but God did grace us with three high school honor grads who participated in various activities throughout their educational journey, went on to obtain college degrees, and are currently gainfully employed. They each have served as mentors to youth in their communities and are generally productive members of society.

So about twelve to fifteen years ago we began entertaining the idea of chronicling what we had learned and experienced over the years. I journaled, noted past events and thoughts for a period, then put it down for extended periods of time, and something would happen, and I would pick it up, jot something else down, and drop it again until the thought would return, or someone might throw the idea out again. The cycle continued. One day I had coffee with a friend and the idea of providing encouragement to teachers and others serving our children through a book arose. The pick it up, take a note, put it down cycle began *again* with that project. Whew, I was tired and frustrated with myself. A book ought to be finished by now, at least one of them.

Enter Melissa Nixon, I think it was the fall of 2014 when I met this Mother Eagle. We were both part of a Women's organization. The group met monthly and each meeting began with a welcome from the chapter's Leadership then each attendee would introduce themselves and share their role in the community. Melissa was one of the leaders. I remember her having us deliver our elevator speeches to one another and then award the winner who captured the essence of the activity. Later in January 2015 she brought these little door hangers and told us to write down our goals for the year. I inscribed 2015 the Year of My

Book. I ran across it recently and was a little disappointed in myself. It has been over three years and the book is just now becoming a reality.

I break the spirit of procrastination, lethargy, and distraction, I move in obedience and with the cloud of my Heavenly Father. My Dreams will not be aborted or miscarried. I will be able to carry to full term and deliver at the appointed time. Exodus 23:26 (NIV)

Melissa and I would connect one-on-one for dinner in November of 2016, five months prior to my 50th birthday. I shared my aspirations of weight loss and authorship. When 2017 came roaring in, I had just received my appointment as Head of School. We were in an accreditation year, so I was busy and I still had no book. But I had begun working on it more consistently. Fast forward to November 2017, I called Melissa, but I don't remember why. She exclaimed that she had been thinking about me. During the conversation she shared that God had laid me on her heart and she wanted to help me get my life together. I was in tears as this was not by happenstance. God loved me and He was illustrating it through Melissa. I contracted with her and the process began. While on that call I shared with her how I had been in four car accidents since August, and I was currently waiting on the police report for the last one at that moment. This conversation reminded me of my Father's love for me, His baby girl, and how I was so important to Him that He would have me on her mind at the precise moment that I called.

When in conversation with others, we are often fueled by their encouragement of our abilities and the confidence in what lies on the inside of us. But then the work must begin, and the roadblock of unproductiveness appears. Melissa and others have called me on this and said, "OK Cheryl, what's the plan? What's getting in your way? What's causing you to be stuck?" I came to the realization that *I* was my number one problem. I was the distraction. I had concentrated on externals; what people would think or say, who would or would not want to hear or receive what I had to say, and if what I had to say had any merit. I was walking in pride and a sense of fear. Pride because I appreciated and, at times, longed for the validation of others to tell me that I was good, I was on the right track, or doing the right thing. In reality, it was not their approval that was needed, but the validation of my Father and His stamp of approval. I needed to be doing what He had purposed and called me to; anything else was disobedience and thievery. Not doing what I have been called to do was me cheating and stealing from those who were the intended benefactors of my purpose. Then there was my fear of the "what ifs" that paralyzed me from any kind of action.

Paralysis is what has set in over the course of the last several years. As I was developing myself for my day job, I failed to make the connection that the very skills I had developed for the classroom were the skills that could transcend the walls of the school. Early in my teaching career, during a PTA event, we had our parents go through the student's schedule as if they were students. Several days later one of my parents contacted me and asked if I would serve as a workshop facilitator for their training company. I agreed to attend one of their sessions. At the end of the session, they asked if I would conduct a workshop in a nearby city. There would be approximately one hundred fifty educators in attendance and I had a week to prepare. I looked at her and her husband like they had lost their mind. My response was, "No, I don't think I am ready for that." I reminded them that their first workshop had eight attendees, yet they were sending me to lead over one hundred. Their compromise was that I would team teach with one of their other facilitators. She would do the first session, I would do the second, and she would close out the day. I agreed, it went well and we began a nearly fifteen-year relationship with my serving the company as an independent contractor.

When I reflect on this event and my coaching conversations with Melissa, I discovered something about myself. The husband and wife team and Melissa were able to see something in me that I had not thought of even venturing into. They asked, and although I was a little apprehensive, I pushed to fulfill their request and I worked hard to represent them. I did not want to disappoint them, nor could I defame their brand. So I showed up for them. My reflection led me to the realization that I needed to show up for *me*. I had to be important enough to Cheryl to make and keep appointments with her. The value that I placed on my commitments to others could not supersede the value I placed on my commitment to me and who God had called me to be. This also takes me to Melissa's book, *"The Courageous Life: How Leap from Your Career to Your Calling,"* in which she explains how we are all carrying babies (DREAMS) that are in gestation well beyond their due date. We have spent years second-guessing our abilities while watching the social media highlights of others, wishing it were us. I declare to you it's Labor and Delivery time! Let's Leap now! Let's give birth to our God-sized dream. We can rest in the Word of God and its declaration that whom the Lord calls, He also equips. Hebrews 13:21 (NIV)

Commitment to one's self must be intentional. During one of my coaching calls with Melissa she told me, "Cheryl you need to be writing every day. You do not have time to chill, play, or go out with friends." When you commit to saying "yes" to you, it may simultaneously mean you have to say "no" to others. We have to be okay with saying "no." "No," is a complete sentence and it does not always need an accompanying apology or explanation. This took a little more work for me. I needed to become better organized. I have a calendar on my phone and iPad, but at times I would make commitments without referencing my calendar or touching base with my secretary. This would result in a serious conflict and unnecessary stress as I scheduled myself for four different events in the space of forty-five minutes on three different sides of town. Having a set plan for scheduling has become a key to organizing and prioritizing my time. I wanted to keep teachers encouraged and to provide a resource to meet this need. Yet, another seed of my teacher devotional. The cycle continues as over the course of the next several years I would toggle between a teacher's resource and a parent resource.

We began the work, but it seemed each time we talked there was something else. My children were going through various growing pains and my husband and I were riding a periodic roller-coaster. Then there were the issues that occurred when transitioning into a new position. With my children, I had to realize that my role had shifted. When they became adults, my role was to advise, pray, and cast every care over to the Lord trusting Him to perfect all that concerns them. I must be Hannah to their Samuel, they belong to Him and I must trust God to be God. In terms of my husband, I had to believe in his love for me and trust the fact that he does not wake up in the morning devising ways to make my life miserable. I also had to make the decision that I would no longer allow negative thoughts to consume me. Negative thoughts and mindsets breed and give birth to worry and fear. But the Word tells me that My Father has not given us a spirit of fear, but of power and of love and of a sound mind (2 Timothy 1:7). I must receive and embrace this because in the past I had allowed my thoughts to wreak havoc in my life. It took my voice and my focus away from my purpose, and much time was lost.

I referenced having had four accidents in the space of five months. The first occurred while I was enroute to a staff meeting that I was to facilitate. No one was hurt, but my car was totaled. Although late, I made it to the staff meeting. Thank God for His divine protection. The second accident when I was returning a loaner car while my new car was being prepared for pick up. We were in the middle of a summer thunderstorm; my car was stopped with the rest of traffic and I was rear-ended. No injuries and we both drove away. Now to the third accident happened on the highway after overnight construction. I saw red lights ahead on my left so I shifted to the right. A few seconds later, there is a car situated diagonally in my lane and there was nowhere else to go but straight ahead. We collided, and my car continued forward toward the center median and my left tires climbed the side of the median, descended, and then came to a screeching halt. Every airbag deployed, the car stopped, yet my Bluetooth was still playing the healing scriptures that were riding to work with me. When it all ended, I heard, he protects all his bones, not one of them will be broken (Psalms 34:20). It is my custom to ride to work with the Word in some form, whether it is through personal prayer, a CD, playing the Word through my Bible app, or listening to ministry via phone. That's my time with the Father. When I heard that scripture I marveled at God's timing and His love for me. He let me know that my angels were on assignment and that He had me. I later found out it was a six-car pileup that extended about three-fourths of a mile. No major injuries again, which according to highway patrol was a miracle. Amen. This car was also totaled and yes, it was a miracle that I did not sustain any injuries.

I was again headed to a staff meeting where we would be receiving Active Shooter Training. I was able to share my testimony with the group and to witness to our guests the goodness of my Heavenly Father.

Now, we all know how inconvenient and time consuming one accident can be…but FOUR! I had to choose to focus on the fact that I was still here, my life was spared, and I was afforded the opportunity to share with anyone who would listen about God's divine protection. This is huge. We get to decide what will have our attention. Yes, I had four accidents and felt the impact in terms of a few aches and pains, but nothing compared to what could have been.

Yes, life is infused with events and situations that can derail our focus and result in the miscarriage of our dreams. The pursuit of our goals will at times require that we have tunnel vision, much like a horse that is fitted with side blinders to safeguard them from the things in their peripheral vision that could catch them off guard, spook them, and possibly endanger their passengers. Distractions are those things in our peripheral. We also can be spooked and lose sight of our assigned course, become derailed, and endanger the babies (DREAMS) we carry. We too must install safeguards that will provide the protection and focused assistance needed in order to get our dreams to the delivery room. This might mean we can't spend time with friends, that the answer is "no", or that a schedule has to established and followed. These self-commitments will help to decrease the negative effects of distractions and result in our increased productivity and the fulfillment of our God-Sized dreams. Identify your safeguards, install the needed equipment, and head to the delivery room...Stat!

Lessons Learned:

- Perseverance births dreams.

- Everyone needs a coach. I needed Melissa, my son, and others to continually remind me of my commitment to me and to push me out of the nest even when I didn't know or believe I had the wings to fly.

- Not everything is a distraction. Timing plays a role as well.

- We must set our focus.

What's next?

Finishing touches to my book are being made and should be completed soon. I look to share this book with others who touch the lives of individuals in teaching, training, or coaching arena. It is my hope that it will encourage, entertain, and empower educators to continue to positively impact the lives of our youth. I also plan to write additional books and share my experiences learned in the classroom and from raising my three children.

Probing questions for you to consider in confirming or accepting your God-Sized dream when overcoming distractions:

1. What distractions are you dealing with right now?

2. Of those distractions, which ones are things that you can control through organization and planning?

3. Which ones are distractions from the enemy and need spiritual warfare such as prayer and fasting?

4. Which ones may be a divine delay?

5. What can you do differently to protect yourself from distractions going forward?

Prayer

Dear God,

I pray for everyone who feels like her destiny is delayed because of distractions. Thank you for showing her the difference between divine delays, plans of the enemy, and when it's things within her control. I thank you for taking these writings and bringing about a shift in our thinking. I declare that our focus is fixed on you and that we see ourselves through your eyes and that we align our thinking and conversation with your Word. Distractions, we will no longer give you place. We are free. We are free from wrong voices, wrong thoughts, and a lack of planning. Father, it is You who orders our steps and we are submitted to your direction. We trust in You and we do not lean to our understanding. Father I thank you that not one vision or dream will be aborted. You are bringing each one to fulfillment in Jesus Name. Thank you for the testimonies that will come as a result. We are excited with anticipation as we expect the performance of your Word in our lives.

We thank you that old things are passed away. Behold all things are being made new in us. Those things that You planted in us, whether it be twenty years ago, ten years ago, whether it was something that was even birthed today, Father God, you who have begun a good work in us, we'll be faithful to perform it. We have our expectations on high alert. We're expecting there to be a performance of your Word in our lives, oh God.

Father God, we're expecting to see the goodness of the Lord in the land of the living. Not in the sweet by and by. We sit down today, and we have a meeting with ourselves. I thank you that each woman will have a meeting with themselves, and with You, and will allow You to speak to them about what that God-Sized dream looks like, and then look at the navigation process. That they will allow You to order and direct their paths because that's what You said you would do in your Word. The steps of a good man, of a good woman, are ordered by the Lord. We thank you that we are free of condemnation. If we haven't done it yet, Father God, today is a new day. Tomorrow will be another new day.

You said that your plan and your purpose for our life is one of good, not of evil, to give us an expected end, a hope, and a future. So, I thank you right now, God, that you're perfecting everything that concerns each one of the hearts of everyone reading this book. Father, I thank you for the dreams that will not be aborted. Your Word says that none will be barren in the land, *nor* lose her young to miscarriage that you are fulfilling our days. I thank you, Lord God, that not one dream will be miscarried, in Jesus name, but each dream will be birthed to its full fruition, in the name of Jesus.

We seek to hear and to receive our direction from You, so that these dreams are realized. And that You will get all the glory! You will get all the praise, and we thank You for it.

In Jesus name,

Amen

Insert your own prayer and/or affirmations for overcoming distractions:

God's Promises

I remain confident of this: I will see the goodness of the Lord in the land of the living. Wait for the Lord; be strong and take heart and wait for the Lord. **Psalm 27: 13-14 (NIV)**

He protects all his bones, not one of them will be broken. **Psalm 34:20 (NIV)**

Being confident of this, that he who began a good work in you will carry it on to completion until the day of Christ Jesus. **Philippians 1:6 (NIV)**

Now on his way to Jerusalem, Jesus traveled along the border between Samaria and Galilee. As he was going into a village, ten men who had leprosy[a] met him. They stood at a distance and called out in a loud voice, "Jesus, Master, have pity on us!" When he saw them, he said, "Go, show yourselves to the priests." And as they went, they were cleansed. One of them, when he saw he was healed, came back, praising God in a loud voice. He threw himself at Jesus' feet and thanked him—and he was a Samaritan. Jesus asked, "Were not all ten cleansed? Where are the other nine? Has no one returned to give praise to God except this foreigner?" Then he said to him, "Rise and go; your faith has made you well." **Luke 17:11-19 (NIV)**

Now may the God of peace who brought again from the dead our Lord Jesus, the great shepherd of the sheep, by the blood of the eternal covenant, [21] equip you with everything good that you may do his will, working in us[b] that which is pleasing in his sight, through Jesus Christ, to whom be glory forever and ever. Amen. **Hebrews 13:20-21 (NIV)**

For I know the plans I have for you," declares the Lord, "plans to prosper you and not to harm you, plans to give you hope and a future. **Jeremiah 29:11 (NIV)**

And none will miscarry or be barren in your land. I will give you a full life span. **Exodus 23:26 (NIV)**

For the Spirit God gave us does not make us timid, but gives us power, love and self-discipline. **2 Timothy 1:7 (NIV)**

I thank Christ Jesus our LORD, who has given me strength, that he considered me trustworthy, appointing me to his service. **1 Timothy 1:12 (NIV)**

Chapter 8

Activate Your Dream

I hope the stories you have read left you full of hope and with a renewed spirit. And that each story has also sparked creative ideas and next steps for your own journey. The obstacles we face along our journeys are not for the faint at heart. No, you are not crazy, and yes, you did hear from God. However, our journeys are for the believer who trusts God to pull them through every time. Obstacles and distractions will always *try* to make you revert to old mindsets and destructive behaviors. But they can only do to us what we allow. They will also try to be vivid reminders of who we are not. However, they never have to reaffirm old lies and belief systems as long as we keep our eyes on the promises of God. The very intent of the enemy is to make us forget who God is and what He has said. Therefore, to recall what God has spoken over your life and your future will always be your greatest weapon for defeating him.

Activate your dream

Let me guess, after reading these stories, you are inspired, right? There isn't any way you can't be inspired. You are ready to either stop procrastinating and start or you are ready to take what you have been doing to the next level. But I know for sure that you are ready to do something. Inspiration is great, but inspiration without activation only produces the same results. It's how we end up going to conference after conference with nothing to show for it. Or how we get to a certain age and wish we had done the thing we always wanted to do ten years ago. Now that your mind has been renewed, let's put everything you have been thinking about to action.

First, I want you to reflect back to Chapter 1 - What's your dream? Hopefully you wrote down your dreams for a number of things. Now, I want you to write down the dream you are going to start or take to the next level today. Only one. More than likely, it's the dream you had in mind when you picked up this booked.

The dream I am going to start or take to the next level starting this week is: (Describe in detail below)

____

____

____

____

____

____

____

____

Write the top 4 things you need to take immediate action on in the next 7 days:

Action:	By When:
1.	
2.	
3.	
4.	

Afterword

Obstacles will not defeat you. Nor will inspirational stories alone sustain you. The biggest thing you can do in pursuit of your dreams is to remember what God said. Remember the promises He said in His Word and in your prayer time about you, your dream, and your future. Reverse replaying what is not right with your life to constantly replaying what His Word says about your life. Do not get discouraged in the midst of your struggles which may have seemed to cause delays. You will arrive to where He desires you to be right on time.

What if we dared to trust God to bring all of our wildest dreams to pass?

What if every time a wild and crazy idea dropped into our spirits, we were full of faith and not fear?

What if our mind and thoughts went to who God is instead of who we are?

Acknowledgements

To Kim, you are the best editor in the land! Thank you for always making me better not only through your service but your support and prayer.

To Lana, thank you for being one of the biggest blessings in my life and always saying, "Yes," in support of my God-ideas.

To Kimberly, you will reach so many sole-inspirers because of your yes to inspire your own soul and share your story.

To Joan, the impact you have and will see is because you were willing to endure your Red Sea moments and share them with others.

To Cheryl, our world and our future are better because of your yes and commitment to our children.

To Nyisha, thank you for saving the ID! That story alone will change many lives!

Thank you, ladies, for your yes to your dreams
and for your yes for this project

Endnote:

"Do It Again" Elevation Worship, Written by George Veikoso / Michael Stevenson / Nicholas Matthew Balding / Christopher Maurice Brown / Mark Kragen / Marc Randolph Griffin / Pia Mia Perez / Jerry Afemata

About the Authors

Melissa J. Nixon

Visionary & Main Author
Keynote Speaker, Consultant, & Trainer

Melissa J. Nixon **prepares, positions and pushes** leaders and organizations to make their next courageous move. The "Courage Coach", as she is called, is known for being a thought-driver and the keynote speaker that will do more than be inspiring. She challenges audiences everywhere to own their voice, show up more powerfully and live by her motto, "I'm not afraid of failure, I am afraid of regret!"

The energy she brings to every stage causes a change in the lives of the audiences. She re-energizes them and breaks down perceived barriers in their thinking. Simple, practical, and real-life scenarios keep audiences engaged and ready to return and take action. There's sure to be laughter, ah-ha moments, and "Yes I can!" revelations. Yes, your audience will be pushed to show up every day as their most courageous self.

She is also the author of *The Courageous Life - How to Leap from Your Career to Your Calling* and *The Profit Playbook for Women – The Ultimate Resource Guide for Building a Successful Business.* **Learn more about Melissa at melissajnixon.com.**

Lana Hunter

Founder, Sundress & Big Hat Brunch

Lana Hunter is the go-to strategist for influencers as well as small businesses. She has a natural ability to create, implement and execute processes and operations, as well as the keenness needed to run events of all sizes seamlessly. Her corporate career spans 20 plus years doing just that for many fortune 500 companies.

After spending years developing and executing strategies that aim to improve the client experiences for many notable companies, Lana took a courageous leap and started a business. Her passion for serving, planning, and creating great client experiences lead her to start this business. Her event planning and business administration skills create amazing client experiences that impact bottom lines.

A native of the beautiful island of Nassau in the Bahamas, Lana loves and lives colorfully. Now calling Grand Prairie, TX home you can find her serving in her community, planning or hosting the next most fabulous event or simply at home with her family and friends. **Learn more about Lana at sundressandbighatbrunch.com**

Nyisha Holliday

Founder, Play to Win, Coach & Speaker

An insightful strategist and passionate motivator, Nyisha Holliday is a Kingdom Success Coach. She helps Christians convert inspiration to manifestation: professionally, financially, and relationally. Nyisha is the CEO of Play to Win University, and the founder of Saved & Wealthy: an online community helping participants achieve financial freedom. Nyisha is an Associate Pastor serving in her church's Bible Institute and Marriage Ministry; a Certified John Maxwell speaker and coach with 20+ in corporate Learning & Development. She is a wife, a mother of three young adult children, and a landlord. Her motto is "You are not chosen in spite of your weakness, but because of it. So don't just play the game, change it!" **Learn more about Nyisha at nyishaholliday.com**

Kimberly Hall

Founder, Sole Inspired

Kimberly Hall, on the surface is a top performing sales professional, who thrives on building solid relationships, exceeding sales quotas, all while driving profitability. As a Sales Director, Kimberly felt empty in a career she wasn't passionate about but did extremely well in. May 2018, Kimberly made a courageous move and started her own business, all while working in Corporate America.

As a runner and lover of scrapbooking and paper, Kimberly launched Sole Inspired, a greeting card company for inspiring, encouraging and empowering others to get up and go, to live a life without regrets, to never back down and to never ever give up. Kimberly's indomitable spirit to beat the odds and take whatever life throws her way, while pushing through the pain to get to her fullest potential, is mostly rooted from the loss of her husband in 2001 and both parents in 2016. She's determined to live a bold, brave and beautiful life.

Kimberly has approached a new season in her life. A season where passion and purpose are the driving force. So much so, she's left Corporate America and is now devoting 100% of her time to growing her business, Sole Inspired. When Kimberly isn't working on Sole Inspired, you will find her running, scrapbooking, traveling the world and spending time with her adult son. Living life in the moment is where Kimberly Hall resides and intends to spend the rest of her days. **Learn more about Kimberly at soleinspiredinc.com**

Joan Turley
Author, Speaker, & Coach

Joan L. Turley is an author, speaker, and coach helping individuals and organizations "turn job hours into joy hours." Her award nominated book, *Sacred Work in Secular Places*, chronicles her unexpected journey out of full-time ministry work and into the secular workforce, ultimately fin-ding her own mission field in corporate culture. Using heart-driven leadership and deep compassion gained through her own experience Joan helps readers, clients, and audience members chart their own course to overcome insecurities and embrace the opportunities God puts in their paths. **Learn more about Joan at joanlturley.com**

Cheryl Riley

Head of School, Victory Christian Center School

Cheryl Riley has spent the last thirty years of her life developing young people. This was something she never saw coming. Her aspirations were to enter the booming technology field. But God had other plans for this lifelong learner. Just as she was about to graduate college with her Mathematics & Computer Science degree, He called her to the classroom. Little did she know this would become her professional home and she would enjoy it. Cheryl loves to see the ah ha lightbulb come on for learners of all ages. Whether it is facilitating a professional development workshop for educators, teaching mathematics to middle and high school students or ministering to an adult ladies Bible class, teaching is who she is and what she does.

Cheryl has a heart for people and is committed to guiding them to reach their fullest potential in every aspect of life. She and her husband, Alvin, live in Charlotte, NC, and have three adult children, Crystal, Dale and Jason. **Learn more about Cheryl at cherylcriley.com.**